TASH LEAM

When Life Gives You Lessons

First edition

ISBN: 978-1-7637994-0-0

To my husband, Jesse.
Thank you for your unconditional love and support.

Contents

Introduction.

I remember the day I turned twenty. I was sitting on my bedroom floor balling my eyes out. I felt… old. My teenage years were over yet I didn't feel like I was any closer to figuring out what I wanted to do with my life. Is this what being an adult is all about? Does everyone else have it figured out except for me? I was single, living at home with my parents and sister in Perth, Western Australia and working in a retail job at a supermarket which I wasn't excited about. I was studying my Bachelor of Commerce at University but I felt like I didn't know who I was or where my life was going. Looking back, I placed a tremendous amount of pressure on myself to have it all figured out.

I can't recall exactly what made me get up off my bedroom floor but I eventually did. I wiped my eyes, took a deep breath in and out and accepted my reality. I couldn't stop the aging process and while things may have felt grim at that point in time, I knew I had a whole decade (and longer) to look forward to. I had heard from older adults that they loved their twenties and it was a time of self-discovery, creating memories and exploring the world as a young adult. That gave me hope.

It wasn't until my mid-twenties when I discovered personal development through a book called Thrive by Arianna Huffington that I found clarity. The book focused on Arianna's recovery from burnout and how she began to thrive by implementing different mindfulness and gratitude practices into her life. That one book inspired me to purchase more books ranging from self-help, self-care, self-confidence and biographies to learn more about the different aspects of personal development. Through these books I learned how to dive deeper into the paradox of who I was compared to who I wanted to become.

I still put pressure on myself to find my purpose and I felt incredibly unfulfilled. By this point, I had completed my Commerce degree and had entered the workforce as an infoline advisor in a public sector job which was emotionally taxing. I was living with my then boyfriend (now husband), Jesse in Perth, Western Australia and I was creating a new home while navigating full time work. I was looking for external validation rather than seeking it from myself. I was trying to live my life according to others. Then slowly, I started to find my own voice and become confident enough to stand up and be myself. I learned to embrace aspects of myself which I couldn't previously including my weight, my values and my spiritual side. I was able to reach a point of self-acceptance.

I feel like I truly reached this point of self-acceptance when I turned thirty. After returning home from an incredible wellness retreat in Denmark, Western Australia a few months after I turned thirty, I felt like I had evolved. I was ready to drop the should's, to create and implement boundaries and to really embrace all that I am. I was no longer craving external validation and I was ready to stand behind the decisions and life I was living.

There's the notion of with age comes less cares. My interpretation of this is that with time, we begin to care less about how others may perceive us and we focus more on nurturing and accepting who we are.

I had heard mixed things about your twenties from people who had lived through it already. Things like 'make mistakes while you're young,' 'you've got time to figure it out,' 'just have fun' and 'your twenties are your pivotal years.' I suppose you could mesh all of the advice together and it would be something like this: have fun while you're figuring it out and it's okay to make mistakes during your pivotal years. Let's face it, everyone's twenties look different, yours will too and that's completely fine. Some settle down early, some enjoy the party scene, others travel, and some are still figuring it out. You can be all of the above and it doesn't mean you're living life wrong. If you're in a different decade altogether, you're allowed to live life on your own terms and do what feels right for you. There's no point in following someone else's life trajectory if it results in you feeling miserable and incomplete.

During my early twenties, one of my main goals was to write a book and become an author. I set myself the goal of being an author at twenty-three and by twenty-seven, that goal became a reality. I self-published my first book, From Human Doing to Human Being in May 2021. Writing the book took several years as I wrote alongside my own evolution. I would try out new modalities such as yoga, meditation or a new morning routine and then form a book chapter around it. It was a way for me to stay accountable to my own personal development but to also take the time to evaluate and celebrate the progress I made. During the time of writing the book, I worked on it sporadically and it was a goal that I didn't share with others. I chose to keep it to myself because I didn't want to be talked out of completing it. I wasn't ready to hear thoughts from others. That book took several years to write and once it was released, I knew I needed to take a break from writing. I wasn't sure whether I'd write another book but here we are.

Once I achieved that goal, I moved onto diving further into my personal development by attending events and learning more about human design and building inner confidence as well as travelling, getting married and starting a candle business alongside my full time job. It felt incredible to become a self-published author and achieve one of the biggest goals I set for myself. Those years since publishing my first book have been filled with trials, errors, and accomplishments. It hasn't always been smooth sailing. Five months after I turned twenty-eight, my grandad passed away which threw me into what I now refer to as The Year I Was a Shadow of Myself.

Three months before he passed, we found out my grandad didn't have much time left. It's hard to know whether it's easier to know someone is going to pass away with advanced notice so you can say goodbye as you want or whether the shock is easier to process. Once I had processed what was happening and about to happen, I got caught up doing the things I thought I was supposed to be doing rather than listening to my own intuition and desires. I wouldn't be surprised if "should" was one of my most commonly used words during that time. While I was focusing on what I should be doing rather than what I wanted to be doing, this period in my life really highlighted it. After receiving that news, I spent most of the year in a fog and not feeling like myself. When my grandad passed away, I felt an immense sadness, nothing I had felt before. While I was glad he wasn't in pain and while I knew he didn't have much longer to live, the morning I received the news, my stomach sank. I don't think anything can prepare you for the grief you'll experience when you say goodbye to a loved one. My heart felt heavy. I felt sad. I was honestly just going through the motions, keeping busy as a way to ease the heaviness. My grief came in waves. I'd be okay one minute and then it would hit hard. There were days when I'd go to work and be crying on the way to or from work. I'd be able to distract myself during the day but then once I got home, I fell apart again. My priorities were rearranged as I allowed myself to grieve and support my family because I discovered everything else could wait. During this time, I learned more about myself, my relationships and who was there for me.

I observed who offered their condolences and provided support to me during that time. I had a few uncomfortable conversations with loved ones to share how I felt about their support or lack thereof. I was strong enough to support others who were grieving but I also wanted those people to ask how I was going, too. Prior to that time, I was okay with harbouring my feelings and not sharing how I felt. It felt liberating to articulate my feelings and to be heard. I was worried it would affect my relationship with my immediate family but it opened up the lines of communication deeper. I also accepted that you may not receive the support you expect from others. When it comes to grief, not everyone knows how to treat you or what they can say or do to be there for you. Whenever you're going through a challenging time, It's okay to communicate what you need or advise others how they can support you.

During this time, I found an inner strength within myself which had been dormant for many years. I could go through hard times and be okay. I also realised that the deeper the grief, the deeper the love. I'll be forever grateful for the times I spent with my grandad, especially near the end. I didn't shy away from him at a time when he needed love and compassion. One of my fondest memories was when I visited him in hospital and we hardly said a word but held one another's' hand. When I offered to get my mum so he could spend time with her, he didn't want to let go of my hand. He said everything he needed to without saying a word. I knew in that moment how much I meant to him, and I him. I'm proud of myself for that, for being there when someone truly needed me. None of us, his family or close friends shied away from saying goodbye. We were there for him, and he knew how loved he always was, by each and everyone of us.

If you are navigating grief, I am sending love your way. Everyone experiences grief differently and I hope you are supported. It may not feel like it when you're in the midst of it, but it does get easier over time. Be gentle with yourself and seek out help, if needed.

One day, when I was scrolling through Instagram, amongst posts on personal development, astrology and human design, I came across a post on Saturn's Return. When I read the post, it made perfect sense, given what I was going through at that time in my life. If you're into spiritual practices, you may be familiar with Saturn's Return. This experience happens every twenty-nine years, approximately around the age of thirty, sixty and ninety. This event occurs a couple times throughout your life with the first occurring between the ages of twenty-seven to thirty-one. Personally, the last few years of my twenties have challenged me in ways I wouldn't have expected, and I think that's been because of the Saturn Return. It provides an opportunity for you to be challenged, to grow and to perhaps deal with lessons you may not have seen coming. Some examples from my life include navigating grief, the end of friendships, changing jobs and beginning to create boundaries in relationships. The side-tracking, challenges and opportunities have taught me some valuable lessons which have provided the framework for this book.

You don't need to be spiritual to be open to the concepts shared in this book or buy into the personal development world. Although, if you have picked up this book, you are probably some way down the rabbit hole into exploring both concepts. We all have times in our life where life feels easy, light and fun. Then, we have the duality of that where we face challenges which are there to remind us of what we're made of (our strengths), what we stand for (our values) and the person we are.

The concept for this book came to me one night. Like many of the wonderful things in life, I didn't go searching for it and it found me anyway. The idea seemingly popped into my head, a download, if you will. I knew what I wanted to name the chapters and the personal lessons I wanted to include in it. When the idea came to me, I started writing because I knew it came to me for a reason.

This book is a self-help book with actionable activities and reflective journal prompts, as well as part biography. I've included examples from my life to help solidify the lessons I've shared in this book. This is the way I prefer to write. I didn't want to write a book about life lessons and not share any examples from my own life. To me, there is a need to be transparent, raw, and real. While each of us have our own journey to embark on with different experiences, I hope that at least one of these lessons or stories shared will resonate with you in some way. I'm not afraid to share examples from my life because it acts as a reminder that we are all going through experiences – good or bad and it's how we learn and evolve. You are not alone, and I want to say a heartfelt thank you for picking up a copy of this book and for being open to learn more. Take what you need and leave what you don't.

Personal development is a broad topic and if I were to define it in a sentence, I'd narrow it down to this: personal development is a continual process, it's a way of life and it offers tools which help you come back to your true self. You may be thinking, do I need to do the work constantly? My answer to that is yes. You may go through seasons where you're well, you're on track and in flow. Amazing! Other times, you may find yourself questioning your decisions and path. In the good and challenging times, it's worth having a personal development practice. Once you begin to create a practice and have tools to help you navigate life, the challenges you face become easier to handle.

Personal development gives each of us tools to navigate the twists and turns of life. Looking back, I have always been drawn to quotes, lyrics, and words which remind me that I am not alone. It's comforting when you hear, see, or read something which reminds you that someone else has gone through a similar situation. Which brings me back to this book. When the idea seemingly popped into my mind, I knew it was time for me to start writing again and to share these lessons with you. The lessons may resonate with you, or they may not and that's okay. This book can be read in parts or cover to cover.

As you read this book, I'd encourage you to not view these lessons as a checklist to be ticked off but rather as a guide. Each of us experiences different things throughout life. You may go through different lessons to learn what you need to, and your journey will look different to mine and others. You may be able to review the lessons, add the prompts to your journalling practice, or find a strategy in the pages of this book to help you deal with a situation you're facing.

The lessons in the book have been divided into three parts. The first group of lessons focuses on separating from our pre-adult life where were dependent on others. The second group focuses on establishing ourselves as our own entity. The third group focuses on growing and evolving as our entity. The lessons throughout the book have been structured intentionally with the hope you'll be able to take notes as you read through the chapter and then use the affirmations, journal prompts and activities at the end of the chapter to take action and solidify what you've learned.

There isn't a one size fits all approach to personal development. It's up to you to take what you can or need from this book and apply it to your life. Think of it as an experiment to see what does and doesn't work for you. You may also find this book helpful if you know someone who is going through a lesson I've shared in this book. It may give you an insight into what they're dealing with and how you can provide support to them, if they are open to it.

For those of you who are just beginning the decade of your twenties, I hope you enjoy them. It's a beautiful period of your life where you can explore, experience, and learn. For those who are in the middle of it, I hope you've been enjoying the journey. Maybe you've entered a chapter where you're wanting to evolve – lean into that feeling and go for it. And lastly, for those of you who are saying farewell to your twenties – what a journey! I hope you enjoyed this decade and I wish you nothing but the best for what's yet to come.

Regardless of where you are in life, I hope these lessons resonate with you. On that note, let's begin with lesson one.

Part One: Separating From Our Pre-Adult Life Where We Were Dependent On Others.

Lesson One: When You Discover What You Stand For.

Clarity of vision created clarity of priorities – John C. Maxwell.

Each of us is born as blank canvas. As we grow, we are shaped by our environment. We learn what is acceptable and what isn't. Our beliefs, values, ideologies, and behaviours are shaped by those closest to us. In most cases, they would be our parental figures. We learn boundaries and how to behave to stay safe. In a sense, we are moulded by others.

Everyone's childhood is different. Irrespective of whether you were an only child or had siblings, your childhood experience is unique to you. Each of us has our own lens through which we view life. Even if you go through the same situation as someone else your experiences will be different. As we move through childhood, many decisions are made for us. Our level of freedom or independence is lower than compared to an adult. Even as you say farewell to your school years, you may already be on a trajectory which has been planned out for you.

If we look more broadly at our external environment, we can see how our culture and society play a part in moulding each of us, too. There are spoken and unspoken rules to comply with if you want to be part of that community. Whether it's within your family, friendship group, or other societal groups, there are norms that you can choose to follow. For instance, if you want to avoid jail, you'll endeavour to be a law-abiding citizen. You learned to adapt to your environment and learn the rules to survive.

If you stray from the rules you'll be treated differently, as an outcast or an outlier. In extreme situations, you may be punished or removed from the group. Using school as an example, there's the popular group and then other subsets. You may crave to belong in the popular group and so you can change parts of yourself to fit in. Maybe it works or maybe it doesn't. I was briefly accepted by the popular group in high school. It was cool until I realised I didn't enjoy being that version of myself and I found another circle of friends to spend time with. If you don't like who you are in an environment, it might be worth changing your surroundings.

At our core, each of us longs for connection and belonging. We are hardwired to be social beings. It's a gift that's been handed down by our ancestors. In earlier times, individuals would need to stick together for safety, warmth, and food. There was safety in numbers. That instinct remains within each of us. While times have changed, a sense of belonging and having meaningful relationships continue to be an important part of life. Loneliness not only feels incredibly isolating, but it also could lead to premature death.

While I don't have the answer for how to cure loneliness, I can offer a few words if you feel like you are still trying to find people who you can connect with on a deeper level. In all honesty, I didn't feel a true sense of belonging until my early twenties. I struggled as a child and teenager to create and foster deep relationships. I would often hide parts of myself to fit in. While I was welcomed into groups by others, I had times when I felt lonely because I chose to hide parts of myself for fear of rejection. I'd show others snippets and when it wasn't well-received, I reverted to the version of myself that they were comfortable with. Upon reflection, it was an act of self-preservation. We adapt to fit in with those around us because we'd prefer to be a watered-down version of ourselves than to stand alone. I'm talking in generalised terms, but I'm sure we've all had a moment in our life where we've chosen to pretend that we do or don't like something because that will make you likeable in that situation.

The fear of being isolated is greater than the fear of not being seen fully. When we reach our adult years, we have more freedom in choosing our environments. We can actively seek out people who may share similar hobbies, thoughts, and ideologies. We can find our people and share parts of ourselves that may have been hidden in the past.

In my early twenties, I realised I was doing things because others were. I jumped into the clubbing scene, had a few too many hangovers, and hung out with people who I didn't particularly resonate with on a deeper level. They were fun and great for a laugh, but we couldn't have deeper conversations. If I brought up a topic other than drinking, shopping or clubbing venues, I was told I was being too serious, and the conversation moved back to something lighter. It was fun at first but after six months or so, I started to yearn for something more. I wanted friendships and connections where I could talk about goals, dreams and the future rather than what our weekend plans were.

Once the novelty wore off, I realised I wanted to find more fulfilling friendships and I made changes. I started to go on day trips, road trips and short interstate trips by myself. Occasionally, a friend would come along with me, but I was more focused on creating space for more fulfilling friendships.

The turning point for me was when I lived in Canada for six months. I had just finished my Commerce degree and resigned from my supermarket job. I travelled to Canada by myself and I took it as an opportunity to be whoever I wanted to be without judgement from others who had known me previously. It was incredibly freeing. It felt safe to show parts of myself that I had previously hidden.

Once I had returned from Canada and settled back into my new work routine, I began to look for and attend events which resonated with me. The events I choose to attend were mainly female based craft events. It was a great learning curve for me because through those changes I met new people who I felt comfortable having deeper conversations with. I didn't have to hide parts of myself and that longing for connection slowly went away. When you can be your true self, it's freeing. You can step wholeheartedly into the light and show all your colours, your strengths, weaknesses, everything. It's vulnerable but liberating.

Sometimes, you need to change your environment to experiment with being truer to yourself. Being with from people who have preconceived ideas about who you are can hinder this process. If you start to act differently, they may lovingly try and get you to revert to who you were because that was comfortable for them.

If you feel like you're ready to create new relationships and show parts of yourself that others may not have seen, it could be worthwhile immersing yourself in new environments. You don't need move overseas solo either. You can look at speaking to different people at work, university, college, events and so forth. If you're unsure about where to start, I'd encourage you to think of something you enjoy doing. Perhaps you enjoy doing craft projects or cooking. The next step is to search for events in your local area and attend one. If you have a person in your life who you would like to go with you, talk to them about it and go from there. You'll have at least one thing in common with the other event attendees which makes it easier to start up a conversation. It may take time before you find a person or people who you connect with but keep persisting. I've met some incredible people and friends at events. You never know where or when you'll hit it off with someone.

When you're able to reveal parts of yourself that you've previously hidden, it's freeing when you find a person or people who embrace those parts of you. It may feel uncomfortable at first to put yourself

14

out there but I promise you, there are people who will love those parts of you. More than this, you'll gain confidence in yourself and become comfortable with just being yourself rather than shying away from who you are.

When you're confident in who you are and what you stand for, life feels easier. Decisions are easier because you can use your values as a decision-making framework. I'll give you an example. Say you're given $100,000 to spend on travel or put towards a house, which would you choose? Both have their advantages and disadvantages. Would you speak to someone else and get their advice on which option you should choose, or would you feel comfortable making the decision yourself?

This is where values come into it. If one of your core values is travel, you'd likely choose travel. However, if one of your top values is security and/or family, you'd likely choose putting the money towards a house. Now what if you choose an option based on what others would perceive to be the best option? If you are indifferent when it comes to travel, but you choose travel because you think others would approve of your choice then you're giving away your decision-making powers. You're also choosing an option that doesn't appeal to you.

If you are still in the process of discovering what your core values are, rest assured you are not alone. I want you to celebrate the fact that you're willing to go on this journey of self-discovery and get curious about who you are and who you want to become at your core. If you are aware of your core values, it may be beneficial to reflect on your current list to see if they still resonate with you.

Below is a table with some common core values. Please note, this is not an exhaustive list. I hope you feel empowered to do your own research to find values which align with you if the ones on this list aren't resonating with you.

Abundance	Acceptance	Accountability	Adaptability	Adventure	Ambition	Authenticity
Balance	Beauty	Boldness	Bravery	Brilliance	Calmness	Capable
Caring	Comfort	Community	Compassion	Confidence	Control	Courage
Creativity	Curiosity	Decisiveness	Dedication	Dependable	Devotion	Dignity
Discipline	Empathy	Endurance	Energy	Enjoyment	Equality	Ethical
Excellence	Fairness	Faith	Family	Fearless	Freedom	Friendship
Fun	Generosity	Giving	Grace	Gratitude	Growth	Happiness
Harmony	Health	Honesty	Honour	Humility	Humour	Imagination
Innovation	Insightful	Inspiring	Integrity	Intuitive	Joy	Justice
Kindness	Knowledge	Lawful	Leadership	Learning	Love	Loyalty
Openness	Optimism	Peace	Pleasure	Poise	Reliable	Respect
Responsible	Security	Self-love	Self-respect	Service	Sociable	Spiritual
Stability	Success	Status	Trusting	Truthful	Wealth	Wisdom

Table of Common Core Values

If this is new to you, spend time reflecting on this. Perhaps some values stand out to you or maybe they don't. Selecting a list of three-five core values can feel overwhelming and it was for me when I first did this activity. Once you select your top three-five values, you aren't stuck with them for life. Your core values will likely change as you evolve and move into different chapters of your life. When you're in your early twenties, your core values may be adventure, freedom, and friendships. When you're in your late twenties, your core values may change to balance, family, and love.

Core values provide a framework for decision making. If you're unsure of whether to say yes or no to an opportunity, you can reflect on whether the opportunity aligns with your core values. If it does and you're excited about the opportunity – amazing. If the opportunity doesn't align with your core values and you don't feel enthused about it, there's your answer. If one of your core values is adventure, you could block out a weekend once a month to go on a day trip or road-trip to explore a new place. That way you are fulfilling your core value of adventure and integrating that into your life. If you value your health, you could create a daily workout routine to prioritise your physical health. You might also prioritise whole foods over processed foods. Remember, clarity yields results.

Knowing your core values helps you create boundaries, routines, and habits. When you know what you stand for you can make decisions with ease.

Affirmations:

1. I am safe to be my truest self.
2. I give myself permission to live my life according to my highest values.
3. I deserve to honour my values and needs.
4. I live and act with integrity.
5. I know what I stand for.

Journal Prompts:

1. Can you think of a moment in your life when you hid a part of yourself to fit in? How did you feel?
2. Would you be willing to shed the parts of you which make you unique to fit in?
3. Why do you feel the need to hide parts of your personality?
4. Are there certain people who you don't feel comfortable being yourself around and why?
5. What is it costing you by not living according to your values? Are you willing to pay that price moving forward?

Activity: Part One: Identifying and incorporating your core values.

Do you know what your core values are? If so, write down your top three-five values. If you are unclear on your core values, use the table above and your own research to write your top three-five values.

Once you've become clear on what your top core values are, it's time to reflect on your current habits, routines, and rituals. For each of your values, journal on this question, 'Am I living according to this value?'

If you are, great! Are there areas in your life where you could level up or expand? If you feel you aren't living in accordance with your core values, that's okay. Acknowledge this and be open to making changes.

Part Two: For the next part of the activity, it's time to identify areas of your life where you can start living in accordance with your core values.

Areas to consider include:

1. Financial
2. Physical
3. Emotional
4. Spiritual
5. Relationships
6. Career Development
7. Personal Growth
8. Life Impact
9. Friendships
10. Romantic relationships
11. Hobbies
12. Travel
13. Further learning

For each of your core values, journal on this question, 'Am I living according to this value in the financial area of my life?' Continue asking this question for each area and for each value. Depending on how you journal, you could create a list and write yes or no next to each value or you can write a detailed response. I want to remind you, just as we have our own core values, your life areas may look different to the ones I've listed above. If that's the case, reflect on each of your life areas and use the list above as a guide only.

Once you've reflected on how you can incorporate your core values into your life, it's time to implement it. If you're after sustainable change, I'd suggest incorporating each idea gradually.

Part Three: Making decisions.

Now that you're clear on your core values, you can use these as a guide when you're making decisions.

Let me give you an example. You've planned a weekend trip, and you've received a call from your boss asking if you can work that weekend. Your trip is next weekend so you still have time to cancel without losing your money. You've identified adventure as one of your core values and while the extra money would be nice, you decide to decline the work because your trip takes priority.

For this activity, I'd encourage you to start making decisions in accordance with a core value. What's a decision you need to make right now or are struggling to make? Write down what you need to make a decision about and the options you've been considering. Once you've written the list, do any of the options align with one or more of your core values? If yes, make a decision based on that option. If there isn't an option which aligns with your values, write one which does and choose that option. It may feel strange to do make a decision based on your values at first but after a while, it will get easier. Remember, you're allowed to make decisions based on what you want to do.

Lesson Two: When What You Resist Most Is Exactly What You Need.

Courage is resistance to fear, mastery of fear, not the absence of fear. - Mark Twain.

This lesson isn't about succumbing to peer pressure or participating in illegal activities. It's about gaining an awareness and an understanding around what you are saying no to and why. When you have an opportunity to try something new do you tend to say no or do you tend to be open to it? If you do tend to say no, do you know why you are resisting something new? Is it a reflex response or do you genuinely have no interest in it?

Our brains crave both novelty and comfort. Our brains like to be challenged and stretched, but not too much. Over time we form our comfort zone, the area in which we feel safe and secure. Our comfort zone encompasses our routines, habits, feelings, behaviours, and activities that we can do on auto pilot and feel comfortable doing. In this zone we feel like we know what is happening and we are confident with what tasks we need to complete each day. It's our metaphorical safety blanket. There isn't risk or uncertainty in this zone because we fill our days with habits and routine and there isn't anything unexpected. We know what needs to be done and we have what we need to achieve it.

The comfort zone is the inner circle when we are looking at the Learning Zone Model. This model was originally developed by psychologist Lev Vygotsky. Beyond our comfort zone we have our learning zone and the panic zone.

The Learning Zone Model

The learning zone is where we can build on our existing skills and capabilities. This is the zone in which we are stretched but not too far that we begin to panic. In this zone you can begin to master new skills. You learn and try new things to see what works and what doesn't.

You may enter this zone if you're asked to take on a new task at work, travel to an unfamiliar destination, try a new cuisine and so forth. The activities and tasks that take you out of your comfort zone and into the learning zone will differ from others because we each have a different starting point. What comes easy to you and the things which are within your comfort zone will differ from others.

Over time the things which were once in your learning zone will become part of your comfort zone. The more that you lean into learning new things and building on your current skills the more your comfort zone expands. The more you enter the learning zone the larger your comfort zone becomes. You can continue to build on the skills and stretch yourself throughout the course of your life.

If the idea of voluntarily entering your learning zone seems daunting, I encourage you to reflect on all the skills you currently have. These were once outside of your comfort zone and they now feel familiar and easy to do.

The outermost zone is called the panic zone. We find ourselves in the panic zone when we venture too far beyond our comfort and learning zones. In this zone, you're beyond what you're familiar with and what you can reasonably be expected to learn. This often results in feelings of overwhelm, panic, and frustration. Just like the experiences that move each of us into our learning zones, the experiences and situations which move us into our panic zone will vary person to person.

When I was twenty, I had my first car accident. I was t-boned at university in a carpark by another driver who didn't give way and drove in what felt like slow motion into my driver's side door. Still in shock, I got out of the car and yelled at the other driver. I was angry but okay. I managed to walk away with a few bruises and whiplash. I knew that I needed to get a photo of his driver's licence and vehicle registration but other than that, I had no idea what to do.

I didn't know if my car was driveable or how to notify my insurance company of what had happened. I was way outside my comfort zone and learning zone. I entered the panic zone. I called my dad and explained what happened. Thankfully, he was working nearby at a jobsite and he power walked his way over to the carpark and knew exactly what to do. He took one look at my car and knew it was a write off because the steering column was completely dislodged. In addition to this, the driver's window had completely shattered inside the door. Thankfully, I had my window down otherwise I may have been cut by glass upon impact. After making sure I was okay and calling my mum to explain what had happened, my dad called the insurance company to organise my car to be towed away and assessed for damage. Once the car was collected, we walked back to my dad's car and drove to a nearby police station where I filed a police report to support the insurance claim.

When the accident occurred, I had no knowledge of the learning zone model. I didn't know I was in the panic zone but I did know I felt out of my depth and needed help. If you have entered the panic zone, it's okay to ask for support. You don't need to have all the answers yourself. After going through the process of what to do after a car accident, I felt equipped to handle the situation on my own, if it happened again.

If you feel like you've entered your panic zone, I encourage you to reflect on the situation that has put you into it. Can you get support from others to help you move back into your learning zone? What is beyond your current skill set and is there a way for you to bridge the gap? How can you reduce the overwhelm and panic? The sooner you can identify that you've stretched yourself too far beyond your capabilities, the faster you'll be able to find out how to leave that zone.

This model acts as a reminder that while it is good to stretch ourselves, there is a limit. That isn't to say that we can't broaden our skill set or learn the unfamiliar. We can certainly learn new skills and acquire new knowledge, but a gradual approach is recommended to avoid entering the panic zone and overstretching yourself.

I want to highlight that while there are times for growth and learning, there are also times in your life when comfort is needed. If you're going through a difficult time such as a breakup, loss of a loved one, loss of a job, or another situation which has a significant impact on your life comfort may be what's needed. Temporarily remaining in your comfort zone will give you space to process your feelings and find your new status quo.

So, what does the Learning Zone Model have to do with resisting things? The model provides us with an insight into human behaviour and our willingness to go beyond our current capabilities and learn something more.

If you tend to stay within your comfort zone, you may be more risk-averse compared to someone who is growing and learning. When you get comfortable in your comfort zone and don't look for ways to expand it, you may also resist new things simply because it is an unknown. You become set in your ways. You're okay with how things are because you have a sense of control. You know what needs to be done, by when and how. You can go through each day with ease because all the tasks are comfortable for you. There isn't anything challenging or out of the ordinary.

If we become too comfortable in this way of living, we find ourselves resisting new things for the simple fact that it is new. Our brain sends a signal saying 'new = unknown = risky = no.' Let's think about someone who chooses to stay in a job they no longer enjoy because they're comfortable. Their tasks, commute, and people they are surrounded by are all known. Leaving that job, even if it means there's an opportunity to enjoy their job again, is more daunting than staying in the role which makes them unhappy. Comfort isn't directly linked to happiness or joy and they stay there because it's safe. They may say things like, 'I just know I won't like it,' 'I'm un-hireable,' or 'What if I don't enjoy it?'

Their fear of something new and unknown outweighs their feelings towards the job.

Our brain doesn't have the processing capacity to weigh up the pros and cons of every decision we make each day. Our brain creates shortcuts (neural pathways) which allow it to filter the information efficiently and make sense of it. The filters our brain uses are unique to each of us. The filters are crafted over the course of our lives and are based on our beliefs, ideologies, and stereotypes we create.

Our brains make assumptions about what we would and wouldn't like to do based on our filters. We form beliefs around our assumptions and these beliefs influence our actions. We can be open to making an informed decision by trying the new thing and deciding whether we like it or not. Or we can make an assumed decision based on our beliefs and past experiences. I have and continue to make informed and assumed decisions although, I do try to make a higher number of informed decisions now.

As I sat on a plane writing this chapter, I had to pause and ask Jesse for examples. I've improved in making informed decisions more frequently that I struggle to think of examples of assumed decisions. I share this as I want to remind you that it's possible to change your mindset and reduce resistance to trying new things, if that's something you're wanting to work on.

For years I painted my own nails because I didn't see the appeal of going to a nail salon to have them done. It wasn't until my sister as my Matron of Honour suggested that she, our mum, and I get our nails done for my wedding. When she first suggested it I was in full resistance mode. I explained how I didn't want fake nails and having an office role, I wanted to be able to type and write without hassle.

My sister patiently listened to my excuses before showing me examples of natural looking nails with subtle colours and styles. During that conversation I tried to be open to the information she shared and

I went with her and our mum to get our nails done. When I sat down and got them done, it felt really relaxing. For two years after that I continued to get my nails done at a salon. I realised it was a self-care practice. It felt nice to spend money on myself and just be still for an hour or so.

I hope you can see how I was resistant to trying something new to the point that I was willing to make an assumed decision until information was provided to me. When the information was provided, I was open to hearing it and taking it into consideration. My high levels of resistance were reduced to a level where I was willing to try it.

I love manual cars and Ford vehicles. My first four cars had a manual transmission and all of them were Fords. After owning my dream car, a Ford Mustang, for two years I felt it was time to get an SUV. Jesse and I started looking at new cars. Being a Ford girl through and through, I looked at Ford SUV's first but there wasn't a model I liked. I also realised that many new cars have an automatic transmission and for years I had held on to the identity of I'll always drive a Ford and it will always have a manual transmission. Jesse found a Mazda which ticked all of my boxes, minus the automatic transmission, and I decided to take it for a test drive. It was love at first drive and I ended up buying that car. After the test drive I was comfortable with letting go of the identity I had given myself surrounding cars.

With both examples my willingness to try something new paid off and it has proven to me the importance of being willing and able to make informed decisions. Now I can have a laugh about it and Jesse just looks at me and smiles when this happens during one of our conversations. I've learned to get curious about my instant resistance to things and to dive deeper into why I'm resisting it. Sometimes, I learn things quickly and other times I need more than a few reminders before I really get it.

If you are resisting something, I'd encourage you to question why. Is it from a belief, story, or identity you hold? Are you willing to challenge what's causing the resistance and be open to something new?

The resistance I am referring to is the type you feel when you don't want to do something because it's new. It's not the resistance you feel when something feels off or unsafe, when something doesn't feel right intuitively. When you say no to things over a prolonged period you may begin to be resistant to new things automatically. It doesn't matter what it is, you'll say no by default because that's what you've trained your subconscious mind to do. If you're open to reducing your resistance levels and feel comfortable saying yes to new things often, you can. You can do this by training your subconscious mind to be open to new things instead of discarding them automatically. This is where you'll need to be aware of the times when you're saying no to something because it's new and overriding your default response by saying yes instead. With time, considering the idea or saying yes to something new will become the new default response.

The next time you catch yourself automatically resisting a new idea, experience, or opportunity I want you to be kind to yourself. Please try to not shame yourself in this moment. Instead treat yourself with grace. The first step is awareness and from there you can begin to question your automatic resistance.

Let's consider that a friend has invited you to a fine dining restaurant to celebrate their birthday. You've never been to a fine dining restaurant. You decline your friend's invitation on the grounds that you don't like the idea of fine dining. Your resistance and subsequent decline of their invitation is based on your assumptions of fine dining restaurants. You have heard people say that the servings are small, over-priced and more like pieces of artwork rather than a meal which will satiate your hunger. You associate fine dining establishments with diners who are well dressed and pretentious. You feel at ease dining at pubs and casual restaurants because that's what you are familiar with.

In this scenario, the resistance is based on assumptions rather than a previous experience.

Now consider that a friend has invited you to a fine dining restaurant to celebrate their birthday. You've never been to a fine dining restaurant. You feel a sense of resistance to saying yes to the invitation because it's unfamiliar and you're not sure whether you'd fit in with the diners who you perceive would dine at such restaurants. Before you accept or decline the invite you research the restaurant by looking at their social media, menu, and website. This has slightly reduced your levels of resistance but you're still feeling unsure. You speak to your friend and ask them why they chose this restaurant and how they feel about fine dining. Your friend explains that they have wanted to dine at this restaurant for a while and thought it would be a fun way to celebrate their birthday with friends. Your friend has been to another fine dining restaurant before and though it's different to a casual restaurant or pub it's a cool experience at least once. Your friend listens to your concerns and suggests that if you or other guests are still hungry after they'll find a dessert bar to go to. Based on this new information you decide to accept the invite and form your own opinion of fine dining restaurants based on personal experience, not assumptions.

Now that you've read through both scenarios, is there one which resonates with you more? If you are currently making more assumed decisions, would you be open to acting like the person in the second scenario?

I hope this highlights that we make decisions differently. There are some topics I know I can be closed minded on however, if someone were to provide new information or a different perspective, I would be open to hearing about it. It wouldn't necessarily change my own opinion, but it may make me willing to consider a perspective, opportunity, or experience I would not have otherwise.

For instance, I don't watch horror movies. It's not a genre of film I enjoy watching and that's based on watching several films from that genre. If someone suggests watching a horror movie I will answer no on previous experience.

If you want to say yes but aren't sure how to overcome the resistance, I'd suggest researching it. Obtain information or talk to someone about how you're feeling about the situation. Just because you try something once doesn't mean that you have to like it or do it again. It means you're open to trying it and from there, if someone asks you about it again, you can say yes or no knowing it's an informed decision.

Before the age of twenty-seven, I'd never been camping other than for a few school camps. Growing up, it's not something my family did. I formed all these beliefs around why I never wanted to go camping. I don't want to go in the bush or dig a hole. I don't want to not shower for several days. I'll get bored. These were my reasons for rejecting Jesse's suggestions of going camping which he respected. It wasn't until one of my girlfriend's suggested that we go camping as a group that I decided to give it a go. She and Jesse both listened to why I didn't want to go and they gave me information which changed my perspective. The real winner for me was, "You don't have to go in a bush. There are toilets available." And we went camping. Now we own our own pop-top caravan and enjoy our regular camping adventures.

There are a few things I want to unpack from this story. First, I created a story around camping which wasn't necessarily based on facts. It felt true for me, but I didn't have any proof to back up my beliefs. Second, I wasn't willing to listen to another perspective about camping. I was stubborn with holding onto my stance when it came to not going camping. It wasn't until someone was lovingly willing to challenge my beliefs and give evidence to the contrary that I was willing to give it a go. Third, I was saying no to something because it was new. I didn't think it would be something I would enjoy so rather than try it and been informed, I decided to not try it.

Perhaps you can recall a time in your life when you've resisted something that you ended up enjoying. While it's your choice as to how you invest your time and energy, if you are saying no to something as a reflex it may be a good opportunity to look deeper. You might just find a new hobby or adventurous activity that you love.

Affirmations:

1. I am open to new experiences.
2. I am open minded.
3. I go with the flow.
4. I allow my perspective to change.
5. If there is resistance, I allow myself to be curious.

Journal Prompts:

1. Why am I resisting this?
2. Is the resistance based on a previous experience or an assumption?
3. How does the resistance feel in my body?
4. Am I holding tension anywhere?
5. Am I open to shifting my perspective on this topic?
6. What are my reasons for resisting this?
7. Am I resisting this because it's new or because intuitively, it doesn't feel right?

Activity:

The purpose of this activity isn't to change your response from no to yes for every decision, it's to help you consider why you're saying no as a default response.

When you default to saying no to something new, take a moment to pause and reflect on why. Why are you saying no? Are the reasons for saying no based on my personal experience or what others have told me? Are these reasons based on facts or a bad experience that is the exception, rather than usual experience? If your default response wasn't no, would this be something you'd consider? What would happen if you said yes?

Lesson Three: Why It's Okay To Be A Work In Progress.

Stop beating yourself up. You are a work in progress, which means you get there a little at a time, not all at once. - Unknown.

The Cambridge Dictionary defines a work in progress as, "something that is being developed or suggested but that is not yet complete."

Perhaps you've been asked the question, "Where do you see yourself in five years' time?" at a job interview or by someone else. Depending on where you are in your life, you may find it easy to provide a response or you may not know. If you don't know where you see yourself in five years' time, that's okay.

You may find yourself looking around at others your age, younger, or older and thinking that everyone else has it together. Everyone else has their life figured out except for me. While it's true that some people are very organised, focused, and know exactly where they're headed, that isn't the case for everyone. If you took the time to ask people if they had it all figured out, I'd guess that many would reply no. Many are working things out as they go along. Others may be closer to achieving their goals than you, but it doesn't mean they have it all figured out.

Life is a series of moments, some of which are anticipated and others... not. While having a plan for your life can be advantageous for having direction and purpose, it may not always go according to your plan. Whether you're going through a period of uncertainty or having to handle unexpected situations, I want you to know that it's okay to be a work in progress. You don't need to have all the answers figured out. Nor do you have to know how you're going to spend every moment of your life moving forward. It's okay to work it out as you go along. Focus on taking just the next action rather than trying to work out how much further you have to go.

Experiment, try new things, and test what does and doesn't work for you. Have fun with life and be its student. Learn what you can, be humble, and be okay with figuring it out. You don't need to have all the answers.

Whether we are aware of personal development or not, each of us is constantly evolving and aging. We are not stagnant beings. Change is inevitable. We can choose to embrace change and accept we are works in progress and that life is a journey (the direction of which is up to us). Or we can resist change and fight to stay as we are.

Recently, I heard a saying that went along the lines of, "When you are twenty you are a one-year-old adult." From the day we are born to when we are around eighteen years old we are given guidance, boundaries, and structures in which to live. We have school, extra-curricular activities, and work to keep us occupied. Yet once we leave school that structure falls away and we are expected to know what we want to do with our lives. It's like we're released into the world and the direction we head is up to us. Some of us know the direction we want to go in. Or at least the direction others in our life expect us to go in. While others may take the scenic route. Some don't move because they're overwhelmed by the vastness of options available to them.

While being a young adult is fun and the possibilities are endless, it can also be daunting and overwhelming. If you are used to having structure and a routine you may begin to feel overwhelmed at the options which are now available to you. Straight out of school you can enter the workforce, begin an apprenticeship, study at TAFE or college, study at a university, start your own business, or take a gap year – just to name a few possible pathways. Not only is there a seemingly infinite number of options to choose from, you're also likely to be influenced by adults around you, your friends, your partner. If you are not careful, you may pick an option which appeases others over yourself, especially if you're not sure what you want to do just yet.

For current and future generations of young adults, social media may also provide inspiration for shaping their future. Before social media existed a persons' world view of what job opportunities were available was limited to what jobs their parents and adults around them had. Social media platforms allow people to see what jobs are available and the qualifications needed to apply for them. This may lead to decision paralysis where you are unable to make a decision due to the vast number of options available to choose from.

Perhaps you knew what you wanted to do with your life after school or maybe you didn't. Maybe you felt the pressure of having to map out your life's path, scared of making a wrong decision. As young adults there is a high amount of pressure placed on us. The world is everchanging and career pathways are always changing and evolving. Perhaps your ideal role or business venture hasn't come into existence yet.

I graduated High School in 2010. I knew I didn't want to go to straight to university to study. I wanted a break, so I took a year off and worked. For me, knowing I wanted a break before studying for another three or four years was an easy decision. What I wanted to study on the other hand, was more difficult. I was torn between two fields of study: media, and hospitality & tourism management. Although my heart was pulling me towards the media degree, I listened to the loving advice of adults around me who said, "You'll have more job opportunities if you study a management degree." Suffice to say, I have a Bachelor of

Commerce degree. While I haven't used my degree to secure a job role, I have applied the skills and theories I learned throughout the degree in my career.

Looking back, I don't regret my decision to study what I did. A lot of the experiences I had at university were pivotal in getting me to where I am now. For instance, if I hadn't had enrolled in the Bachelor of Commerce degree, I would not have discovered the thrill of going on a road trip by myself or gone on a working holiday to Canada. In one of the units, we were required to go on a road trip to study tourism in a regional area. I chose to go to Bridgetown and it was my first solo road trip. I enjoyed the experience and learned that I could travel by myself and still have fun. If I had studied a media degree, I would not have gotten that opportunity.

Now I realise that I didn't need to figure out the trajectory of my life in that very moment. I could be a work in progress. Arguably, we are all works in progress. We are constantly changing and evolving, whether we want to admit it or not. Life does not remain the same, even if we do.

After I graduated, I lived and worked in Canada for six months. I knew I wanted a break and to celebrate my hard work over the past three years. I knew if I didn't go then, I would likely never go. That trip allowed me to be me and to have some invaluable life experiences. By me, I mean I was able to immerse myself in a new environment where no one had any preconceived ideas or expectations of who I was. I had the freedom to be my whole self. Some may consider a working holiday to be a waste of time or a detour from starting a career. I saw it as an opportunity to travel, gain life experience, and fulfil a dream.

I felt the pressure to return to work straight away once I returned home so I reached out to my former employer before I'd left Canada. I had a job waiting for me when I got home. The idea of being without a job scared me at the time because I felt like I would be letting people down if I didn't start employment right away. Once I was back home and working again, I felt like I had it together. I had my fun in Canada and now it was time to be an adult.

The pressure of feeling like I had to have my life together returned in my mid-twenties with a vengeance. I was reading self-development books and learned about the concept of having a life's purpose. I became hyper-fixated on trying to work out what mine was. I was a drawing a blank and in hindsight, putting way too much pressure on myself. I felt like everyone in the world knew their life's purpose and I was the outlier. Jesse was able to help me shift my perspective on the topic when he lovingly reminded me that I didn't need to find my purpose to make an impact or live my life. I wasn't failing at life by not knowing what my purpose was in that moment. I equate the pursuit of purpose to trying to catch a butterfly. If you chase butterflies, you likely won't catch one but if you stand still, one may land on you. Sometimes, we need to pause and let the answer come to us rather than trying to force it.

What does having your life together mean and look like to you? Is it attaining a certain lifestyle, starting a family, getting married, landing your dream job, travelling the world, having financial freedom, or something completely different?

Just like success, the phrase "having your shit together" is highly subjective. I can guarantee that my definition is different to yours and throughout your life your definition will likely change. If I could tell you why we feel this innate need to have our lives figured out and our shit together, I would. The truth is, I'm not entirely sure. It could stem from children when we are asked, "What do you want to be when you grow up?". It could be a story we've created and tell ourselves daily or it could be a perception that everyone in the world bar you, has their shit together. If you do feel pressure to have your life together, it may be beneficial to set aside time to reflect on why that is. If you aren't wanting to reflect, that is more than okay. You don't always need to reflect on something before moving forward. However, identifying where the belief has stemmed from may help. You know yourself best, so please do what is right for you.

I had planned on staying home only for a few months before heading back for a second winter season in Canada, but my plans changed.

After I returned home I was dumped by the guy I was seeing. I was insistent on staying single, but life had other plans. Shortly after I met Jesse. Not having been in a committed relationship before, I thought I'd still be okay with going back to Canada and we could just have a long-distance relationship for a while. That didn't happen. I still remember the day I sat on a park bench with Jesse feeling torn about what I would do. We'd only been dating for a few months but I felt like I was falling for him. As much as I wanted to go back to Canada, there was a sinking feeling in the pit of my stomach. That feeling was my intuition's way of telling me, "If you go, you'll regret it." It was one of the strongest intuitive feelings I've experience to this day and I am grateful that I listened to it. I decided to stay in Perth and see where the relationship would go. If the relationship didn't work out, I knew I could always book a flight to Canada.

This change in plans meant I needed to figure out other parts of my life. Where was I going to live and was I happy in what I thought would be temporary job? I put a lot of pressure on myself to start figuring out the answers to these questions. I started to feel overwhelmed by all the choices I felt I needed to make. In addition to these decisions some of our friends were starting to get engaged, married, pregnant, and buying or building their own homes. While I didn't want to be settling down or living a life like theirs, I did want to have an idea of where my life was heading. I began to compare myself to others and I truly felt like I was nowhere near having my life together at twenty-three.

I got caught up in feeling like what I was doing wasn't right or enough.

I had defined "having my shit together" as buying a house, getting engaged then married, having a full-time job, and settling down to start a family. I can tell you now, I was not ready for most of those things. I had created a definition based on what others were doing and what I thought I should be achieving too. I was ticking things off that list such as moving out of home and trying to find a job I enjoyed but I wasn't close to thinking about marriage or kids.

Jesse and I got engaged when I was twenty-five and were married two years later. Tick. I had managed to cross off a few items on the getting your life together checklist. I decided to give myself more time and so I told myself that I'd have my life together by thirty. That gave me time to redefine what "having my shit together" looked like so by the time I turned thirty, I had dropped the pressure to have anything together at all. Now that I'm in my early thirties, I've taken the pressure off myself to have it all figured out. I'm okay with being a work in progress. I realised that I do have my life together. While it may not measure up to someone else's definition, it measures up to mine and that is all that matters.

There have been times when I felt that I lacked purpose in one or more areas of my life. I equated this with not having my life together. What I didn't consider with this way of thinking was that life changes. Not every chapter of your life is going to be smooth sailing. There are highs and lows. We are human after all.

I felt like I was blindly following society's definition of "having your shit together" without questioning it until I entered my mid-twenties. It was then that I realised I wasn't ready to settle down or think about having a tiny human. I wanted the freedom to travel, experience life and be okay with moving on to another workplace if that one was no longer serving me. Living in accordance with my values, and prioritising my well-being and needs felt good.

You don't have to have it all figured out. Sometimes you do.

Sometimes you're still on your way. Other times you have no idea what you're doing. All are valid places to be in and often there's a reason for being exactly where you are.

You are allowed to be a work in progress. Period. Life happens. Whether it's the death of a loved one, a worldwide pandemic, a job loss, breakup, financial crisis or another trauma there are times in our lives when something happens that we didn't see coming. These moments allow you an opportunity to reevaluate your priorities and the trajectory of your current path. You're allowed to figure it out as you go along and make changes as needed.

There are also times in your life when your priorities change abruptly – either temporarily or permanently. It's okay to grieve the person you were before the event and to feel a little lost as you enter the new reality. Remember, you're human. Personal evolution comes with gains and losses. You're allowed to grieve for the parts of your life that are no longer.

This next story involves the death of a loved one so if this is something you're currently going through or processing it may be best to turn the page.

At twenty-eight, my grandad passed away. It wasn't unexpected but for a while he was going okay. Until he wasn't. It felt strange grieving someone while they were still here yet that was what I was doing. When he did pass and we were all grieving, a part of myself was relieved he wasn't in pain or a shell of himself anymore.

In the month leading up to his death and for a few months following, I was in a daze. My grief felt like a wave hitting the shore. Sometimes it was calm and manageable, but at other times it felt all consuming. I gave myself space to feel the emotions as they surfaced which wasn't easy, but I knew I didn't want to suppress them. During this time, I was also waiting to start a new job, starting an online business, and offering support to my loved ones.

Emotionally, I was spent but I kept going. I focused on putting one foot in front of the other. For the rest of that year I kept pushing on, telling myself what I should be doing. I was getting frustrated that I wasn't seeing the results I wanted because I wasn't able to do what I thought I should be doing to get those results. In hindsight, I was out of touch with who I wanted to become. I had defaulted back to following the crowd rather than making my own path.

The following year, at age twenty-nine, I decided that I had enough of how I was feeling. It was time to find a way out of the haze. It was time to get back into my routines and work out who I wanted to be moving forward. I dropped the things I thought I should be doing and focused on what I wanted to do. First that meant getting clear on my goals, priorities, and core values. It also meant dropping the shoulds and the feeling of needing to have my life together.

As I reflected, I realised how much time energy I spent on the shoulds. I wasn't necessarily acting on the shoulds either. It was more of a thought, "I should be doing this." Followed by inaction. It occurred to me that if I felt I should be doing something and I wasn't, then it wasn't the right thing for me. Sometimes it feels easier to blame everyone else for where you are in life but if you want to make changes, it's on you. To be the master creator of your life you must be accountable for your actions. There's not much point in dwelling on what has happened because that's done. It's best to invest your energy and time into the current moment because the things you do today will have a direct impact on your future.

If I caught myself saying I should do this, I'd dig deeper. Why did I feel like I should do this? What belief did I have that makes me feel I should do this? Who am I trying to please? If you notice you're should-ing yourself, get curious about it. The way we speak to ourselves says a lot about us. Should reflects something you don't really want to do.

When you realise the shoulds aren't aligned with your goals, values, or beliefs it's time to get clear on what does align with them. And how can you stop doing this should activity?

I started an online business in network marketing because at first, it felt like a great fit. It wouldn't take much time, there was an opportunity to earn money, and the potential to make it a full-time job. I jumped on the team chats and learned more about the business, but I wasn't consistently doing the work of speaking to people to share about the product and benefits. I kept telling myself for months that I should work on the business and speak to people, but I didn't. My strategy was to share information about the products on social media and let people come to me. I wasn't prepared to sell directly to anyone.

Eventually I decided to stop the business because it wasn't the right opportunity for me. I wasn't prepared to do the work required or suggested by those who had made this opportunity their livelihood. I couldn't get past the limiting belief I had of speaking to people and promoting the product. It just didn't feel right. It didn't align with my values.

Once I made my decision to stop the business, I felt relieved. To someone else looking in at my life it may have looked like a failure. In my reality it was a great reminder that not all opportunities are suited to you. I tried it and it didn't feel right. In that moment, I could have told myself that I didn't have my life together and this was another example of that. Instead, I choose to feel grateful for trying something new and learning so many things in the experience.

We've covered a lot in this chapter, and I want to leave you with this takeaway. When you live life according to your own values and embrace the ups and downs of life you will always have your life together, even when it may not feel like you do. Take the pressure off yourself and keep making progress towards your goals, self-development, and growth. Everything will fall into place as it meant to.

Affirmations:

1. I am a work in progress.
2. I am an action taker.
3. I am focused on my own goals and aspirations.
4. I am living life at my own pace, on my own terms.
5. I am constantly evolving.

Journal Prompts:

1. What is your definition of having your life together? Is this definition based on your own beliefs and opinions or what you feel is expected of you by others?
2. Do I feel like I need to have my shit together? If so, why?
3. If you feel like you don't have your life together, what do you want to focus on? What do you feel is incomplete or missing?
4. When has this feeling surfaced in my life? What was going on for me during that time?
5. When I look around at loved ones and acquaintances, do I believe they have their lives figured out? Why or why not?
6. Do I know where the need to have my life together has come from?
7. What would having my life together look like? Is it attainable right now? What steps can I take towards it right now?
8. Why do I feel like I don't have my life together? What am I doing to the bridge the perceived gap?
9. At what age do I expect to have my life together? Why?

Activity:

Find a space to sit down and spend 15-30 minutes to complete a brain dump. Write down any words, experiences, or things you associate with having your life together. Write down whatever comes to mind, without judgement. The aim of the exercise is to bring forward thoughts from your subconscious mind. Once you've completed your brain dump, look at what you've written down and see if any of the words resonate with you.

From there, you can choose to journal on the words that don't resonate with you to see where they've come from. Are they stories you've created or things you've heard from others? You can also look at the words that do resonate and evaluate how you can work towards attaining them.

Lesson Four: You Can Bring Out The Best Or Worst In Someone.

When we seek to discover the best in others, we somehow bring out the best in ourselves. - William Arthur Ward.

Whether it's a platonic or romantic relationship, you can shine a light on someone's strengths or you can focus on their flaws and contribute to the diminishment of their self-worth. The same goes for those who you allow near you, they can bring out the best or worst in you.

You're allowed to be selective when it comes to who has access to you. You're allowed to remove yourself from situations which no longer align with the version of yourself that you'd like to be. You're allowed to thrive and not just survive. The same goes for how you're treating others. If you are bringing them down or keep clashing, it might be time to try and improve the relationship or part ways.

When you're around a person or group of people who have a negative outlook on life or seem intent on bringing others down, it can be taxing. You may begin to doubt your own abilities, have a negative outlook on life or treat others as you're currently being treated. While we cannot control how others treat us, we can choose how we interact with others and who we want to be around.

I want to be clear that the purpose of this lesson is not to identify who is at fault or to blame others for how they exist in the world.

Instead, I want to highlight the importance of choosing who you surround yourself with. Through my own experiences of friendships and relationships, I have learned to appreciate the ones where I can be my better self while also giving space for the other person to be their best self too. These are the relationships where we feel safe, trusted and loved. That isn't to say that we may not find ourselves surrounded by people who have a different outlook on life.

If you are more of an optimistic person, you may find it taxing to be around people who are pessimistic. There's a conflict of perspectives and while you may spend your time trying to get them to change their outlook, you'll eventually be brought down to their level or at minimum, to the middle ground. The roles may be reversed, and it could be you who is pessimistic. If you're surrounded by optimists, it may feel overwhelming. Your mood may shift over time, and you may begin to adopt a more positive outlook however, there's a chance that you'll be bringing down the energy of others to achieve a new status quo.

In contrast, I've been in a relationship where I have acted out, was passive aggressive and intentionally tried to hurt the other person. When the other person did something which hurt me, I'd do something in return. The trust they placed in me was something I used against them to hurt them whether it be by sharing personal information (in the form of gossiping) or doing something which I knew would hurt them emotionally. Looking back, it wasn't a healthy relationship but at the time, it felt like it was everything I wanted. It was only after we broke up and I left the environment we were in that I realised how I didn't want to be that version of myself in a relationship. I wasn't my best self, and I/they deserved better. Instead of being a team, we chose (whether consciously or subconsciously) to be divided. We chose to hurt each other in return rather than discuss our feelings and be vulnerable. It was a pattern of behaviour which neither one of us was prepared to break or even aware of, at the time.

While I was living in Canada, we had a tight-knit community. Many of us who lived together in the shared houses worked at the same ski-resort. We were living in a small town and we stuck together. A few months into the trip, new people arrived and joined our circle. There was a noticeable change in the dynamic of the group. Many of us began to gossip about who was seeing who, amongst other topics. Many (not all), members of the group adjusted their behaviour to fit the new dynamic. I was one of them. I began to gossip and focus on the drama. In my lousy defence, there wasn't much else to do. After a few months, I realised how much my behaviour had changed and I pulled back from certain members of the group. I no longer wanted to be part of that dynamic. It was then I realised, we can bring out the best or worst in others and vice versa. It wasn't a specific individual, it was the situation. I adapted to fit the situation rather than changing the situation to suit me.

During these times in my life, I didn't have any knowledge of personal development. I wasn't aware that personal development was a practice nor how many resources were available. I can't change the past and without this lived experience and epiphany, I may not have reflected on who I was vs. who I wanted to be. While I am not proud of how I behaved in both situations, both afforded me the chance to hold a metaphorical mirror up to myself and to reflect. If we want to move forward and make progress, we need to be okay with facing ourselves, being honest and accepting what has happened.

Upon reflection, I was able to observe previous patterns of behaviour and acknowledge that I haven't always taken the high road. I have been nasty, malicious and vindictive. I have intentionally wanted to hurt others emotionally when they've hurt me. At the time, it felt easier to hurt them and give them a taste of the pain they inflicted on me than it did to sit down and have a conversation. Hurt people can choose to hurt others or they can choose to stop the cyclic behaviour and choose differently. During my early twenties, I wasn't willing to choose differently. I was okay with stooping to someone else's level of behaviour to prove a point. The two stories above were pivotal points where I realised I didn't want to be that version of myself anymore. Even if you're hurting, it doesn't mean you have to inflict hurt onto others.

When we are interacting with others we can choose to respond or to react. If you are around someone who wants to get a reaction from you, you may feel like you're in a reactive state most of the time. Being around someone who is negative or diminishes the worth, skills, or strengths of others is emotionally taxing. The effects of having such a person in your life varies depending on your ability to disregard what they say, your level of self-worth, other relationships in your life (Is this type of person an outlier or a common type of person in your life?), and the length and depth of the relationship (platonic or romantic).

If you feel like you have been surrounded by this type of person and are unsure how to leave the situation, you may want to confide in a trusted person or seek professional help, depending on the severity and impact it is having on your life. Either way, choose someone who you trust and provides a safe space for you to talk openly and honestly to create a way forward. Letting go of a relationship isn't easy, but neither is holding onto something that is causing you, and possibly the other person, pain. Pick your poison.

When I was twenty-seven, I enrolled in a mindset course which shifted my perspective. I was able to see where I was reacting, playing the victim and not being accountable for my actions. It was a group coaching course and over the period of six weeks, with the support of others in the group, I was ready to choose differently. It wasn't always easy and I still have moments where I'm tempted to act rash and react, rather than respond. What helps me in those moments is to visualise the possible outcomes. I picture myself in the situation where

I react and create a little story of how the other person may respond to my behaviour. Once that scenario plays out, I create another story in which I respond and imagine how it will be received by the other person. From there, I tend to choose how I respond in the real-life moment. I'm proud to say that the majority of the time I choose responding over reacting.

The key here is the majority of the time. We are human and there will be days in our lives which will test us. You could have all the self-awareness in the world yet if you're running on minimal sleep and your cortisol levels are high you may not have the cognitive ability in that moment to respond. Your only option might be to react. If you are wanting to be someone who responds rather than reacts to a situation, to be the best version of you as often as possible, give yourself grace. Catch yourself where you can and choose responding over reacting. When that isn't feasible, try to not feel ashamed or guilty. Work on repairing the situation if it warrants it and if you would like to and move on. All of us have off days so give yourself the compassion you extend to others.

Before moving on, I want to define what I mean when I refer to the term best version of you or best self. I define best self as the version of you who acts according to their highest values. They're self-aware and accountable for their actions and behaviour. They control their energy and don't engage in gossip. They choose to uplift and support others. Your definition of your best self may vary from the one I've shared here. It's a subjective topic and you're allowed to define it in a way that aligns with you.

While it may feel like it at times, you are not stuck in situations. You can move on. If you are in an environment where you are surrounded by people who are on a different trajectory to you or have a completely different view on life, I want you to reflect on whether you're in the right environment. People and environments can raise our vibrational frequency and encourage us to do and be better, such as reaching our goals, dreaming bigger, and having a more expansive outlook on the world. Or they can diminish our self-worth, our confidence, and make us feel like we are too much. They can make us feel like we need to stop being ourselves.

When you're around a group of people you may feel uplifted (positive energetic state) or drained (negative energetic state). There may have been times in your life when you've entered a group and something felt off. This could be due to the energetic state. It may not always be appropriate to change the energetic state. At a funeral there may be a sombre feeling throughout the room due to grieving the passing of a loved one. The wake may be more spirited and uplifting while people laugh over shared memories and celebrate that person's life.

At other times it may be necessary to try and change the energetic state. If you're the coach of a sports team you may need to offer some inspirational words during timeouts. If the team are losing to the opposition their mood may need to be lifted to help them focus on the game and appeal to their desire to win. There's not a one size fits all approach to this. It's important to learn to read the room, the current energetic state, and whether it needs to be adjusted. It doesn't have to be your responsibility to regulate the energetic state of the room. However, it is useful to pay attention to it.

If you don't want to change the energetic state but also don't feel comfortable around the group, you can choose to leave. You can choose who you surround yourself with and while it may be hard to leave a group of people in pursuit of finding others who are better matched, it's possible and worthwhile. You don't always need to remove yourself from an environment. You could choose to enter it less frequently or make changes to see if that alters how you feel in the environment.

Remember, you can surround yourself with people who support and uplift you or you can be surrounded by people who keep you small, dismiss your abilities and take you for granted. A question to ask yourself: Does this environment bring out the best or worst parts of me? How am I contributing to the environment? What parts of myself am I showing and giving to others? Do I want to stay in this environment?

While it may seem easier to point the blame at others in the environment or metaphorical room, doing so removes your accountability. You will need to be open to reflecting on your behaviour. Are you contributing to the current energetic state or are you trying to change it? It may feel confronting to reflect on your own behaviour. However, it isn't a one-way street. For change to happen, you'll need to take responsibility for your behaviour and evaluate what you want moving forward. It's near impossible to change others. If you focus on trying to change yourself you may be able to affect change, but you cannot force someone else to change.

Now that we've considered the energetic state of the environment and groups of people you're around, I want to focus on individual relationships. There are people who you connect with almost instantly and others you clash with. You don't have to like every single person you interact with and vice versa. You can choose how you interact with people you don't like. Whether the dislike is on a personal or professional level, you can choose to be civil.

You can try and treat everyone with kindness and compassion, or you can alter your behaviour depending on how you feel about the person. I believe it's possible to act civil towards people we don't like on a personal level. They don't deserve to be treated with disrespect or hurt simply because we don't like them. It also takes energy to harbour dislike or hate towards someone so if you can aim for indifference, you aren't investing any extra energy into the relationship.

Just as you'll encounter people you don't like, there will be those who don't like you. If someone doesn't like you, that's their choice.

You don't need to take it personally and make changes to who you are to try and convince them to like you. My recommendation is to put your energy and focus into relationships which uplift and support you. Focus on finding people who you connect with, value and can be yourself around.

Affirmations:

1. I choose responding over reacting.
2. I am kind, caring, and compassionate.
3. I am here to support and uplift others.
4. I am mindful of how and where I invest my energy.
5. I choose to act in alignment with my best self.

Journal Prompts:

1. Do I treat people I don't like differently to those I do like? How?
2. Do I notice the mood in the room? Do I add to it or try to change it?
3. Do I improve or detract from the mood of a room?
4. Do I believe I can change others? Why or why not?
5. Am I okay with being disliked?

Activity:

Write down the names of 3-5 people you are closest to and the name of someone you dislike. Next, write down some words that describe your relationship with each person on the list. How do you treat them? How do you resolve conflict? If they needed your help, how would you support them? Once you've completed the list, I want you to compare how you treat those you like with those you don't. Is there a massive difference? Are you comfortable with how you treat them?

Lesson Five: When You're Tempted To Be An Asshole.

"I feel like life would be easier if I was an asshole but I don't want to be."

These were the words I uttered to Jesse when I was twenty-nine and in the middle of the Year I Was a Shadow of Myself. I was emotionally worn out. It was a year that tested my ability to be kind and patient with others. It was a year of change, grief, and feeling lost. I felt lost in who I was and the direction I wanted my life to go in. There were people who I thought would offer support and, in my eyes, they didn't. It was a compounding effect of feeling like I was giving to others when I had nothing left to give and it wasn't reciprocated. Instead, they wanted more and I couldn't give more than I already was. I felt ready to put myself first and stop giving parts of myself away to others.

While I had been focusing on trying to put myself first for a few years, this was the catalyst for change. I had enough of appeasing others at the expense of my own time, money and/or energy. Being emotionally worn out forced me to make changes now because I knew I couldn't keep doing what I was. I evaluated how I was spending my time, energy and money. I looked at my relationships, including the one with myself and evaluated if I was spending too much time or too little time on them. I made the decision to block out time on the weekends to spend with Jesse and our dog, Lana as well as implement some additional self-care activities such as nature walks, yoga and writing.

My sense of self was tested in different areas of my life including my relationships, friendships, and at work. I was trying to do a lot of things to appease others and I was reaching my end point. I realised I needed to communicate my needs better, be okay with saying no more often, to avoid being a people pleaser, and be true to myself rather than lowering my standards or behaviour to adapt to the situation. This year showed me that I needed to treat myself better.

In most situations you have two choices: respond or react. I prefer to respond, yet I was getting tempted to react and act petty. I was tired of feeling like I was getting taken advantage. Rather than reflecting on why I felt that way, I wanted to act like an asshole. At that point, I wasn't ready to reflect on my actions that had led me to be in this situation. Some of those actions included: a lack of boundaries, repressing my feelings, and creating space between myself and others when needed.

Due to a lack of boundaries and poor communication, I was allowing people to walk over me. I was giving them time and energy that I didn't want to and I was feeling resentful. Rather than addressing the issue by creating a boundary or communicating with the person, I wanted to act petty instead. As much as I wanted to act out, I didn't. Instead, I chose to withdraw and not communicate how I was feeling with others. I bottled it up and pictured situations in my head where I acted like an asshole and realised it wasn't worth behaving in that way. That left me with two options, continue to be withdrawn or address the problem head on.

During this time, I was trying to build my online network marketing business from the ground up. Rather than using social media content and captions that were provided by leaders, I wanted to create my own. I noticed that others started to use my content without permission which irritated me. I began to focus on whether they were getting customers and enquiries based on my words. I noticed that one person was continuing to use my content and after 5 or so posts, I decided to send them a message to address the problem directly. While I was tempted to act petty and call them out on it publicly, I knew I'd feel better if I addressed it directly with them. I asked them to stop using my content without my permission and to their credit, they did, which I appreciated.

The person didn't realise their behaviour upset me and once I brought it to their attention, they apologised. While I waited longer than I could have to address the problem, I refrained from acting petty. I grew tired of feeling irritated and complaining about the problem and it was at that point that I decided to address the issue.

Perhaps you've been through something similar. If you have or are going through it now, please try to avoid stooping to the level of others. It isn't worth it. Try to focus on you and find ways to replenish yourself. There will be things we go through in life which test us. During those times give as much as you can to yourself to avoid the risk of hitting emotional burn out.

An asshole is essentially a person who is self-centred, rude, and obnoxious. Life may seem easier if you're an asshole because you are looking out for your best interests only. It doesn't matter who gets hurt or offended in the process. If you are getting your way, you're okay.

If you are a typically kind person and are tempted to start behaving like an asshole, I encourage you to sit down and think about what is making you want to act out in this way. What do you need? What do you want to stop doing? Who do you feel is taking advantage of you?

Rather than succumbing to acting like an asshole, you can look at what's causing you to want to act in this way and then take positive action to avoid it. When you can start to understand the reasons behind your behaviour you can start to make changes. Perhaps you need to distance yourself from people, say no to additional tasks at work, or start prioritising yourself again. It could be a combination of all three things or something different altogether.

Wanting to behave like an asshole could be an indicator that you're outgrowing the life you're in, the people you're surrounded by and/or the environments you find yourself in. In a work environment, when I've grown tired of the job or feeling like I've been overworked, I tend to notice a change in my behaviour. In a previous job, I was trying to complete the tasks of three-four people due to lack of staff. This increased workload continued for months and after a while, I felt myself harbouring resentment towards other people in the team. I felt like they only had one job to do and they weren't willing to take on additional tasks to support the team or lessen my load. While the people I was working with didn't say thank you or take on extra tasks, it was noticed by senior staff who took the time to express their appreciation. That simple thank you lessened my resentment temporarily and I decided that the situation wasn't going to improve and it wasn't sustainable for me to be working at that level for much longer. I didn't throw my hands up and quit but I did start to look for other jobs.

In this example, I didn't act like an asshole although there were days I was definitely tempted to call in sick or quit. Instead, I realised that my environment needed to change as the staffing levels weren't going to improve anytime soon based on communications from upper management. I took positive action by applying for jobs and when I was successful, I was able to hand in my letter of resignation.

You may feel stuck in these situations but there are options available to you. If you can find a way to look at the situation rationally, you can decide what your next step is whether it's conversation, letting go of a relationship, finding a different job or changing your environment. You don't need to be stuck in a state of resentment or frustration nor do you need to act like an asshole.

Affirmations:

1. I am kind, caring and compassionate.
2. I am aware of my environment and the impact it has on me.
3. I am allowed to remove myself from environments which no longer serve me.
4. I seek out others who support my growth and evolution.
5. I continue to level up and grow.

Journal Prompts:

1. Where in my life am I feeling resentful?
2. What do I do when I'm feeling this way?
3. Am I open to changing my default response?
4. What can I do to avoid feeling resentful?
5. What's my definition of a nice person?
6. What's my definition of a kind person?

Activities:

1. Reflect on a time when you want to be petty or act like an asshole How did you refrain from acting out this way? Did you notice yourself changing your patterns of behaviour or mindset to not act petty or like an asshole? How did you act in that situation? Were you remove yourself from that environment? How did you feel after the situation? If you could turn back time, would you handle the situation differently or the same way?
2. Reflect on a time when you were petty and acted like an asshole. Why did you choose to act in that way? Did you consciously decide to act that way or was it an impulsive response? How did you feel after the situation? If you could turn back time, would you handle

the situation differently or the same way?

Lesson Six: When It's Time For A Relationship To End.

You have to let people go. Everyone who's in your life are meant to be in your journey, but not all of them are meant to stay till the end. - Unknown.

The year was 2010. There was a gymnasium filled with Year 12 students who were about to graduate high school. A PowerPoint presentation with photos of friends, teachers, and events played on the screen. The song *Friends Forever* by Vitamin C played through the speakers. Around the room there were smiles, laughter, eyes filled with tears, and a hint of sadness. I was eager to graduate high school and move onto the next chapter of my life. While it felt bittersweet for such a long chapter of my life to be ending, it was exciting too.

For many, it was a time of uncertainty. How would friends keep in touch? How would everyone's lives change? Would we be friends forever? Or was this the end of a friendship? No one had answers. Promises, assurances, and plans were made following the graduation ceremony. How many were fulfilled, I can't be sure. One thing I did observe was my fellow graduates were scared of not being as close to their friends anymore. Or worse, losing a friendship.

Maintaining friendships at school was easy because you had the opportunity to see each other five days a week. You were in the same location and even if you didn't have classes with your best friend or friend group you could still catch up before, during, and after school. You may have even lived nearby making it easy to hang out during the school holidays, after school, and on weekends. What would happen when the dynamics changed? When everyone was going off to work, college, or university? Would they create new friendships and leave behind their school friends? Only time would tell. Personally, many of my school friendships ended in my early twenties. We grew apart and formed new friendships.

For those who are in their early twenties, you may be experiencing this now. If you had a close-knit friend group through school, you may find that you begin to drift apart as everyone moves into adulthood and gets a job, travels, undertakes further studies, etc. You may find you form new friendships as others begin to fade away. If you're sad about the loss, allow yourself time to grieve. Letting go of a friendship or mourning the change of going from best friends to acquaintances can hurt because you have fond memories and a lot of love for the time you shared together. Treasure those moments and know that you'll be able to create more in the future, even if it's with a different person or group.

Throughout your twenties and throughout your life, you will have different friendships and relationships. Some may last for most of your life and others for a season or a shared experience. Not all relationships are meant to last a lifetime. Sometimes you grow apart, grow up, or find others who you can relate to more. You may be in different seasons of your life and the common interests you once shared are no more. Regardless of the length of time every relationship has meaning. When a friendship or relationship ends, it doesn't mean you've wasted time investing in that friendship or that it didn't mean anything. An ending doesn't signify wasted time. It signifies the closing of a chapter and the opportunity for a new beginning. While you may not have any tomorrow's together, no one can take away the yesterday's you shared.

While most relationships go through phases, it's important to know when to let go. Some people are only meant to be in our lives for a chapter rather than the whole book. Letting go often comes with mixed emotions because goodbyes or creating space between you and someone you were close to is an adjustment, but sometimes it's needed.

There are situations which will test relationships. Some situations include the loss of a loved one, a new relationship (platonic or romantic), the end of a relationship, starting a family, and moving away – to name a few. You may find that you're not the friend you want to be in these situations or that you're not supported by your friends in the way you were expecting.

Another situation which may test your relationships is the personal development or evolution of yourself or others. You may utter or hear the words... You've changed. A person you once knew deeply may become an almost stranger. Each of us change as we move through life. Whether it's a physical, mental, or emotional shift change happens. It may leave us questioning this new version of a person we thought we knew completely. Or it may leave us feeling like we've lost them for good. There are infinite reasons for why people change, and it could be due to a positive or negative influence. If you are concerned that a loved one is changing due to a negative influence it's up to you if or how you intervene.

When I began my personal development journey, I really struggled to find people who I could connect with. I assumed that the people around me weren't interested in personal development and so I didn't engage in conversation with them about the topic. Many of my friends at that time weren't on the same journey and I didn't feel comfortable talking to them about my newfound passion. Our conversations stagnated and I found myself yearning for new relationships. In these circumstances there was absolutely nothing wrong with the other person. I still held them in high regard. I just felt that we didn't connect as we once did.

Our interests and reasons for connecting in the first place had changed. I didn't end friendships and relationships. However, I did make a conscious effort to create new ones with personal development as the foundation.

There are times when the common interests you shared with someone are no longer enough to keep the friendship going. The friendship may end completely or it may be downgraded from best friend to friend, or friend to acquaintance. While it can happen organically there are times when a friendship or relationship ends abruptly. "You've changed" or "I don't know who you are anymore" are phrases that often get thrown around during such situations. Whether you're on the receiving end of those words or the one speaking to them, it is not your responsibility to remain the same person. You are allowed to change and evolve as you see fit, as is the other person. While it may be tempting to revert to your old ways of being to keep the status quo, I want you to consider the cost of doing so. If you're reverting to your old self you are likely forgoing your own development for the benefit of someone else who isn't ready to see you change. You do not need to remain the same person to appease their perception of you.

If your lives are headed in different directions your relationship has a few options. You can recalibrate and find a new status quo, accept the status quo as it is, or part ways. It's okay for relationships to run their course. When you can acknowledge and accept that not all relationships are meant to be for the length of your life you can make space for new people.

If you are growing as person, you may reach a point where the behaviours you once accepted are no longer acceptable to you. At this point, it could be worth creating a boundary. To do this, you can have a conversation with the person or people involved and from there make your decision. You could let them know that you don't accept this type of behaviour anymore and what the consequence is if it continues.

Depending on the outcome the friendship could continue, you might reduce your investment in the friendship such as the amount of time spent together, or you may choose to end it. Not everyone deserves to get full access to you and if someone isn't willing or able to acknowledge and take responsibility for how their behaviour is affecting you and the relationship, you can choose what to do next.

While this chapter has focused primarily on friendships and platonic relationships, the questions above can also be used when reflecting on romantic relationships. Whether you're single, in a new relationship, or in a long-term relationship, romantic relationships require work. The work I'm referring to is effort that should come from both people in the relationship. While there may be periods when one person carries the relationship (for instance, during a period of grief), it isn't sustainable for a prolonged period.

We each have our own values when it comes to relationships. What feels good for one person may not to another. I value reciprocity, mutual respect, support, and compassion. I like to feel supported and to support my significant other. While we remain individuals with our own hobbies and interests, we act as a team. We have personal and shared goals that we are working towards. What you value may be similar or completely different to what I've described and that's normal.

I encourage you to reflect on what you value in your romantic relationships. What kind of partner would you like to be and what kind of partner would you like to have? What does the dynamic of your relationship look and feel like to you? If there are gaps in your current relationship and where you want to be, it may be advantageous to have a conversation with your significant other and see how they feel about the relationship. Perhaps the relationship already fulfils their needs and they're unaware of what you feel may be missing or could be improved.

While I'm not a relationship expert by any means, I do believe that a core part of any relationship, whether it's platonic or romantic, is trust and communication. As much as we'd like others to be mind readers, it's rarely the case. If you have an unmet need or feel something could be improved, speak to them. No one knows you better than you, even your significant other. It's unfair to expect them to know what you're thinking or wanting all the time, regardless of how well they know you. Clear and consistent communication is a great way to nurture your relationship. Discuss your needs and listen to the needs of your significant other too. Afterall, communication isn't a one-way street.

Before I met Jesse at twenty-two, I had a few short-term relationships. Most of the time I was the one to end things. The main reason I chose to end the relationships was when I realised we weren't compatible. I couldn't see myself moving through life with them by my side. I felt like my feelings for them weren't going to develop into anything greater than like. Once I had this realisation, I would find a way to end the relationship so that I wasn't preventing the other person from finding someone who could love them unconditionally, in ways I knew I never could. Hurting someone in those moments wasn't easy but I knew the longer I stayed in the relationship feeling the way I did the more hurt it would cause them in the future. Goodbyes are hard but holding onto something you're ready to release is harder still.

Once you can acknowledge that not all relationships are meant to last a lifetime you can start to value what you have on a deeper level. Rather than assuming it will never end and taking it for granted, you can find ways to appreciate the special moments and celebrate what you have while it's yours. It also gives you the freedom to let go of what is no longer right for you or the other person.

Affirmations:

1. I allow space to create new relationships.
2. I allow relationships to end in their own time.
3. I value all my relationships.
4. I choose to be giving, supportive, and kind in my relationships.
5. I seek out relationships that are fulfilling for both people.

Journal Prompts:

1. If you sense a relationship is changing or coming to an end, how do you react? Do you try to hold onto it, or do you accept that it's changed?
2. Do you find it difficult to create new relationships?
3. Do you have space in your life for any new relationships?
4. Do you prefer to have many friendships or a few closer friends?

Activities:

1. Reflect on a time when a friendship or relationship ended. How did you feel? Did you grieve the relationship, or did you accept that it was over? Did you try to replace the relationship, or did you take time to tend to your other relationships?
2. If you're going through a challenging phase in a relationship, you may want to ask yourself "how do know whether a relationship is meant to last or if it's just for a chapter?" You can reflect on how you act and feel around the person. You can also reflect on the questions below:

- How do I feel and act around this person?
- Do I look forward to interacting with them or am I filled with mixed emotions?
- Do I feel like we have a balanced relationship where we support

one another? If not, what can I do to improve this?
- Do I feel like I am giving more to the relationship and not receiving (or vice versa)?
- Is our relationship growing and evolving or have we stagnated?
- What do I value most about the relationship?

Lesson Seven: When You Know, You Know.

And when your heart knows, it knows. There's no explaining it. You can only trust it. - Evan Sanders.

Have you ever had a feeling that you can't put into words, yet it just feels right? That's your gut instinct or intuition at play. You may have experienced a moment in your life when you've felt pulled to do something. It was a feeling you were unable to articulate. It may not have made much sense to yourself or others, but it just felt right. I call it the 'when you know, you know' feeling.

We often make decisions from our head rather than our heart or intuition. We write out pro and con lists, seek out the opinions of others, and spend a great deal of time weighing up our options. On a subconscious level we may feel it's irrational to decide on a (perceived) whim. Yet... when you know, you know. Making decisions from our head affords us the ability to explain and justify the decisions we make to others. We have physical or tangible evidence to put forward, should we be asked for it.

Decisions made from your heart or intuition do not allow you to present such evidence. You could say something along the lines of, 'it just felt right' or 'I felt called to make this decision, I can't explain why.' It may leave people who are seeking evidence of your decision-making process baffled or with more questions, yet that is not your concern.

Not every action or decision you make needs to be justified, especially to others.

When Jesse and I were planning our wedding, we looked at several reception venues. The venues were nice but if we booked one of them it would have felt like a compromise. There was something not quite right with the venues. Either the price, the venue, or the food didn't appeal. They were great options, but we weren't sold on any of them. A few weeks later we visited Acquaviva on the Swan. We walked along the jetty, pulled open the door, and as soon as we stepped inside the venue, we looked at each. Without saying a word we knew this would be our reception venue. For both of us it was a full bodied yes. From the glass to ceiling windows, the blue and white interior, we both felt at home. I could instantly picture us walking through the doors on our wedding day and being greeted by a room filled with our loved ones.

This happened again when I went dress shopping. I ended up purchasing my dress from the first shop I visited. One of shop assistants recommended a dress to me and as I put it on... it felt right. The dress had pockets and the name of the dress was Gemini. Gemini happens to be Jesse's star sign. Funnily enough, most of our wedding decisions were made using that guidance. We trusted our intuition and it turned out to be a beautiful day.

I share this because if you aren't used to making decisions from your intuition it may feel like the decision hasn't been thought through. It may feel impulsive, irrational and somewhat irresponsible – either to yourself or from those around you. If you find you are judging yourself for deciding from your intuition I encourage you to reflect on where those beliefs are coming from. Are they self-imposed or from others? Chances are we are judging our own decision-making authority and it almost feels like a shortcut if we don't spend hours agonising over a decision. I also encourage you to reflect on who you're making the decision for. Is it for yourself or for others? If you're doing what is right for you there is no wrong way to make that decision. Your intuition has your best interests at heart.

Call it what you want but our intuition is powerful. It's our internal compass which aims to keep us safe. Just as you know when you know, there are times when you may feel unsafe and are unable to put it into words. That empty, sinking feeling or dis-ease you feel is likely your intuition telling you something is wrong. What you do with that feeling is up to you.

One night I was at home by myself while Jesse was interstate for a work trip. Around eleven at night, I had a sinking feeling in my stomach. A feeling I had never experienced before or since. Prior to the sinking feeling, I was lying awake in bed, trying to fall asleep without success. My border collie, Lana was in the room with me, and she was restless too. When the sinking feeling happened, it was such a strong feeling that I got up and called my parents. I realised I didn't feel safe being in the house that night and I needed to leave as soon as possible. I asked if Lana and I could stay at theirs for the night and when they said yes, we jumped in the car and headed off a few minutes later. I didn't bother packing a large overnight bag, I just headed over with Lana in my pyjamas. I don't know what the outcome would have been if I had stayed at the house but I am glad I didn't stay around to find out.

Sometimes, our intuition feels like a whisper and other times, it can be fiercely strong. It is up to you whether you want to tune into your intuition or not. If tuning into your intuition is something you haven't really done before, it is a learned skill. You can begin with consulting it on small decisions and build up from there.

To start tuning into your intuition you can become aware of how your body feels when you're deciding. Do you feel your body tensing up or is there feeling of relief or stress being released? When you're deciding, do you feel resistance in your body, stomach, or mind? If so, get curious about what the resistance means and listen to your body.

Not all decisions need to be made based on your intuition. However, if you have times in your life where you feel like you're at a crossroads or feel overwhelmed by the number of choices available leaning into your intuition can help. It is free of the stories, beliefs, and thoughts of others that our logical mind often considers when making decisions.

When I've truly taken the time to head the guidance of my intuition, I've been okay. The environments I removed myself from or the decisions I made were exactly what I needed in that moment. In contrast, there have been times when I've discarded the guidance from my intuition and things haven't worked out.

Remember, we don't owe an explanation as to how we've come to a decision to others. It can be as simple as trusting that when you know, you know – irrespective of how you came to that conclusion. Feeling like I owed others an explaination was the biggest barrier stopping me from leaning into my intuition more frequently in my early twenties. I thought it was better to be pragmatic and painstakingly agonise over decisions – big and small. I wanted to have proof of my thought process and how I came to the decision I had when asked by someone else. Using your intuition or head to make decisions is equivalent to working out a mathematics equation. Some can do the working out in their head, so when the answer is alone on the paper people wonder whether they cheated. Others prefer to show their working out on paper so all can see how they got to the answer they did. Even if both reach the correct answer, one is often questioned more than the other. Use the process that works for you.

Affirmations:

1. I am guided by my intuition.
2. My intuition has my best interests at heart.
3. I trust my inner knowing.

4. I am open to making decisions based on my intuition.
5. My intuition is here to support me and keep me safe.

Journal Prompts:

1. What is my definition of intuition?
2. Do I feel like I listen to my intuition frequently?
3. How does my intuition speak to me?
4. Am I open to listening to my intuition?
5. What does a yes from my intuition sound and feel like?
6. What does a no from my intuition sound and feel like?
7. Write about a time when your intuition was strong in a bad situation.
8. Write about a time when your intuition was strong in a good situation.

Activity: Additional Guidance for Using Your Intuition

If you find yourself overwhelmed with the options available, I'd encourage you to find a quiet place and be still. Allow the noises around you to become quiet, as you tune into yourself. The world around you can wait. You are exactly where you need to be during this present moment.

I want you to think of the decision you are pondering. How does your body feel? Does it feel heavy, tense or weightless?

What thoughts fill your mind? Are your thoughts concerned with how others may be affected by your decision? Are you worried about disappointing someone else? Are you putting the wants of others before your own? Do you know what you want to do but are unsure because it's in conflict with the expectations of those around you? What does your intuition say? What does your head say? Are they giving you the same or different answers?

If you knew you were supported by those around you regardless of the decision you made, what would you choose? Is there a conflict between your head and intuition? Which are you hesitant to listen to? If you are listening to the logic of your mind, how would it feel if you chose that option? How would it feel if you listened to your intuition and leant into that choice?

Do you know what your decision is? Can you stand behind the decision or are you hesitant? What is stopping you from making a decision? How long have you been pondering the options?

With this process you can journal on each question individually or use it as a guided meditation to help you move through the thoughts and feelings in your body.

The purpose of the guidance is to assist you in engaging with your intuition. Your intuition will likely feel different to mine and those around you because each of us are unique. It's about familiarising yourself with the sensations and ways in which your intuition is trying to interact with you. Even for big decisions you often know what you need or want to do, even if it defies logic. That's your intuition at work.

Part Two: Establishing Ourselves As Our Own Entity.

Lesson Eight: When You Release What You Can't Control.

"Instead of worrying about what you cannot control, focus your energy on what you can create." - Roy Bennett

Accept the things you can control and let go of the rest. It sounds simple, right? Yet, many of us try to control the uncontrollable. There are numerous things in life which are beyond our control. It doesn't matter how diligently we stick to a routine; things happen. Uncertainty is a part of life. Each of us has a level of uncertainty which we are willing to tolerate. When we surpass that level, that's when feelings of stress and discomfort begin to appear.

I used to struggle with unforeseen circumstances such as delayed flights, cancelled plans, or inclement weather on a day when I was hoping for sunshine. I've come to accept that there are variables in life that are beyond my control. I prefer to focus on what I do have control over rather than what I don't. I shifted where I focused my thoughts and energy which reduced my stress levels and overthinking. Even when you try to account for every possible outcome, there will always be more.

This shift didn't happen overnight. It took time to adapt to this new way of life, but it is possible. There's a sense of inner peace that comes with embracing what happens and knowing that whatever the outcome, you've done all that you can. If a situation hasn't turned out as you expected, it's okay to feel how you do. The aim is to move through those emotions to find a way to adapt to the new situation. We cannot change what has happened, but we can learn from it and keep moving forward.

The situation which solidified this for me was when Jesse and I planned on getting married in September 2020. We were engaged in September 2019 when I was twenty-six years old and we held an engagement party to celebrate with loved ones. Then we started to think about the kind of wedding day we wanted to have. We sent out our save the date cards to invited guests and organised most of the vendors including the ceremony and reception venues. We were proud of our efforts because we managed to have everything organised in two months, by the end of January 2020 to be exact. When the pandemic hit in late March 2020 everything became an unknown. Life seemingly changed overnight and we realised that our plans were about to change, whether we wanted them to or not.

By mid-April 2020, we made the decision to postpone our wedding for one year in the hope that it would allow our interstate guests to attend and for there to be no restrictions on guest numbers. I can still recall Jesse and I standing in the kitchen, torn about what we would do. Would we try and risk it? Or, would we make the decision to postpone and hope the pandemic would be over by then? Making decisions based on an uncertain future is incredibly challenging. I don't often wish for a crystal ball but in that moment, I definitely did. Part of me knew that we needed to postpone but another part of me wanted to wait it out and see if it would all work out. I'm glad we made the decision we did, even if it meant waiting another year to walk down the aisle and marry the love of my life. After we made our decision, I set about reorganising our wedding. Thankfully, our vendors were compassionate and available the same day the following year. It took about two weeks to have the new wedding day planned.

While we were able to get married in 2021, interstate guests were still unable to make it due to travel restrictions. We were sad that some of our loved ones couldn't make it for reasons beyond all our control and yet we accepted that it happened. Our only other choice was to postpone the wedding a second time but neither of us were prepared to do so.

This situation taught me the importance of being flexible with plans and to focus on what I can control. We couldn't have foreseen a worldwide pandemic hitting months before we had intended to get married, yet we needed to find a resolution. We went into problem solving mode by reaching out to our vendors and cross-checking their availability. Our original wedding photographer was non-responsive so again, we needed to be flexible. We found another photographer who captured our day perfectly.

In this instance, our day turned out better than either of us had envisioned. Was it stressful rescheduling everything? Yes. What would have been more stressful was if we were indecisive and avoided thinking about whether to postpone the wedding and hoping it worked itself out. We had no way of knowing whether the decision to postpone was the right one, but we made it regardless.

I think it's fair to say that many, if not all of us have had situations in our lives that haven't unfolded as anticipated. In these situations, you can spend time dwelling on what has happened and thinking about how unfair it is, or you can accept what has unfolded and find ways to focus on resolving the issues. You can choose acceptance over resistance.

Acceptance of a situation doesn't equate to liking what has happened. It simply means you've accepted it and from this position, you can focus on moving forward rather than trying to control the uncontrollable. Resistance on the other hand, prevents you from moving forward because you're trying to change what has already happened.

As Coco Chanel has been attributed with saying, "Don't spend time beating on a wall, hoping it will transform into a door." The faster you can accept what has happened, the quicker you can find a solution and way forward.

Acceptance is how you can get your personal power back. It allows you to build resilience, to look for solutions, and to embrace the change. You can focus on working through the challenge rather than resisting it and wishing it didn't happen.

Acceptance means acknowledging that the situation has happened and knowing you'll find a way to deal with the obstacle, problem, or challenge. Acceptance gives you an opportunity to learn and move on. You cannot move forward if you're constantly looking back.

Things don't always go according to our own timeline, yet it all works out when it's meant to. If you can find a way to balance taking action and trusting it will happen when it's meant to, you'll likely begin to feel calmer. You'll find you're no longer trying to force things to happen because you're willing to trust it will happen. What is meant for you will find you.

As humans, we crave safety and security. Either at a conscious or subconscious level, we believe that if we can have complete control over a situation that we won't be harmed. Trying to control yourself, others and your external environment is impossible – not to mention exhausting.

Think about it. We try to change others rather than change ourselves because we believe it's easier for them to change. We try to change or control the external world in which there are so many variables we will never have full control over. Perhaps that realisation scares you or maybe it allows you to feel calm. Thinking of everything that could happen or trying to control all the possibilities is an exhausting feat. Instead, you can focus your attention on what you can control and release what you can't.

We cannot control how people respond to our actions. We cannot control what happens during a worldwide pandemic. We cannot control the weather or the traffic jam on the way to work. We can shift from being in a reactive state to a responsive state.

When you begin to accept that there are variables in life that we cannot foresee or control, you can learn how to move through life's highs and lows with ease. Rather than focusing on the what if and trying to predict how each situation or interaction is going to unfold, you can focus on how you show up, the effort you put in and allow the outcome to be what it may. Relinquishing this level of control isn't easy at first but I'd encourage you to try it.

You may be wondering, what can we control exactly? In one word, ourselves. Each of us can control how we show up in this world. We can choose how we interact with others, what we take accountability for, what our core values are, and what we spend our time, money and energy on. We can control how we perceive a situation and how we show up each day. By showing up, I mean the energy you bring (emotions), how you present yourself (appearance) and the actions you take. You have control over yourself, embrace it.

When I was learning to shift my focus to variables within my control, I would say 'it is what it is'. This phrase reminded me that the situation has happened, and I cannot change it. It may not have unfolded in the way I hoped or expected but I have the option to go with the flow and move forward rather than dwelling on what didn't happen. During this time, I felt like I had more control. I reduced the number of things I was thinking about such as possible outcomes, and I was able to focus more on what I was doing. I reduced the time I spent thinking of different outcomes and shifted my focus to what I could control… taking action.

If we equate life to a river, we can either float through the water, navigating the twists, turns and obstacles by going with the flow. Or we can choose to fight the current by resisting change, the flow, and the obstacles. It begs the question, which person would you prefer to be? The one who floats along, going with the flow and allowing what will happen to happen. Or the person who resists change and spends most of their time and energy fighting the current?

There isn't a right or wrong answer to this question. I feel like many of us have been both during our lives and it depends on the situation. Asking yourself this question allows you to determine how you would like to use your time and energy. As Socrates once said, "The secret of change is to focus all of your energy, not on fighting the old, but building the new." If change happens unexpectedly, you may not be ready to accept or embrace the new situation. You may need to process what has happened before you can accept it. You may want to resist the current for a while before you're willing to go with the flow.

An unexpected loss, grief, or even a win may throw us off course. It takes time to move through the emotions, process what has happened, and move forward in your new reality. It takes time to adjust so if you find yourself getting frustrated or feeling like it's taking longer than you thought it should, please give yourself grace.

Going with the flow doesn't mean you're always happy about the challenging times or endings. What it does mean is that you're accepting of what is happening. Rather than resisting the situation, you accept it for what it is and move forward.

When we were twenty-nine, Jesse and I decided we were ready to purchase a house together. We had been living together since we were twenty-four in the house Jesse bought and built and now we were ready to find our next chapter home. It was time to close the chapter on the current house and begin a new one, together. My days of not having a mortgage were about to come to an end! We discussed the amenities we wanted in the house, the location, price, and size of the block. We had a good idea of what we were after and with that framework, we began to go to open houses. We wanted to get an idea of what we would be able to get for our allotted budget. Some of the houses we looked at were not our style and then there were several we put offers on.

Waiting to hear back as to whether our offer was accepted or not was suspenseful. When we found a house we both liked enough to put an offer on, we felt excited and nervous. When the offer was being considered, it was challenging to focus on anything else but there was nothing we could do except wait. When the offer we submitted was not accepted we felt disappointed and a little disheartened, but we didn't give up. We knew that the house for us was out there. We just had to keep searching. We didn't see the rejected offers as a reason to stop searching, we saw it as an opportunity to keep looking.

During the process, we met a real estate agent at a home opening who showed us a house we really liked and put an offer on. We were certain our offer was going to be accepted but another offer was accepted instead. At that point, I felt defeated. I started to believe we weren't going to find a house after all. Thankfully, the real estate agent hadn't given up and they showed us a house which was off the market. It was exactly what we were after. After we walked through the house, we decided to put an offer in on the spot. The real estate agent had the paperwork prepared and the owners agreed to our offer and signed it that night. It worked out better than we had imagined and we hadn't even considered buying a house off market. If I had tried to predict every outcome, I would have missed that one. Which is why it can be advantageous to keep an open mind and trust that you'll reach the outcome, even if you can possibly imagine how.

I share this experience because throughout the process we had people who told us: it was the wrong time to buy, there weren't many houses on the market, it would take months to find something. Along with the naysayers, we also had supportive people in our corner who knew we would find a house. The process of selling Jesse's house then buying and moving into our new place took roughly three months. Given houses on the market were selling at a rapid rate, we were proud of ourselves for doing what we did in the time frame we did it in.

We couldn't control whether our offer would be accepted. We could control going to open homes, looking at what was available on the market, and persevering. In time, we found the house that was right for us and I'm glad the other houses we put offers on fell through.

Chances are, you've experienced something similar in your life. If you haven't yet, I'd encourage you to ask others to share their stories with you. This will help you to reshape your story around this lesson and will provide social proof that it's possible.

If you find yourself in a high stress situation, take a moment to pause. Reflect or write down what you can control in that moment. Are you worried/anxious/stressed/overthinking things that you can or can't control? If you're focused on what you can't control, it's time to find a way to let it go.

If you're wanting to focus on what you can control but aren't sure how, try the following approach, and make changes as needed:

1. Identify the differences between your expected outcome vs. the actual outcome of the situation.
2. Of the differences, which factors are inside your control and which are outside? List these out in two different columns.
3. Which factors have you being trying to control? Highlight from each column.
4. Reflect/journal on what it would look like if you focused solely on the factors within your control.
5. Begin to focus on the factors within your control. If you feel yourself wanting to focus on something outside your control, remind yourself: "I release what I cannot control."

The purpose of this approach is to help you determine what you're focusing on. If you go through the process and identify that you're spending most of your time trying to control factors outside of your control, it gives you an opportunity to shift your focus. For instance, if you're trying to control the past or future, you're missing out on the present moment. Sure, you can reflect on the past or plan for the future however, the best way to shape the future is to make changes in the present moment.

Letting go of what you can't control is challenging at first but with time, it becomes almost second nature. You begin to sift through the variables of a situation to sort them into categories of what you can and can't control. When you can accept that there are things outside of your control, it frees up mental, physical and energetic capacity to focus on what you can control and make progress forward, past the current situation.

Affirmations:

1. I release what I cannot control.
2. I surrender to the outcome.
3. I choose to focus my time and energy on my actions rather than variables beyond my control.
4. I can control my thoughts, feelings, and actions. I allow the rest to unfold as it will.
5. What is meant for me will find me.

Journal Prompts:

1. Do I tend to go with the flow, or do I like to control the situation?
2. How do I feel when a plan doesn't turn out as anticipated?
3. Am I open to change or new opportunities?
4. Am I willing to try and relinquish control in an area of my life?

Activities:

1. Reflect on a time where you tried to control the outcome. How did the situation make you feel? If you had relinquished control in that situation, what do you think the differences would have been?
2. Reflect on a time where you went with the flow and trusted it would work out. How did the process feel? Was it easy, challenging or another feeling? How did you feel once it happened?

Lesson Nine: When You Fail, You're Learning.

Don't fear failure so much that you refuse to try new things. The saddest summary of life contains three descriptions: could have, might have and should have. – Louis E Boone.

Mistakes and failures are a sign that you are trying new things and making progress. You cannot have success without failure. It's part of the process. Noone is immune to making mistakes or failing at things. In her book "Rising Strong", Brene Brown speaks about stepping into the arena. Brene writes, "I want to be in the arena. I want to be brave with my life. And when we make the choice to dare greatly, we sign up to get our asses kicked. We can choose courage or we can choose comfort, but we can't have both. Not at the same time. Vulnerability is not winning or losing; it's having the courage to show up and be seen when we have no control over the outcome. Vulnerability is not weakness; it's our greatest measure of courage. A lot of cheap seats in the arena are filled with people who never venture onto the floor. They just hurl mean-spirited criticisms and put-downs from a safe distance."

The arena is the place where people try new things. People who are on the outside of the arena are defined as life's bystanders. Throughout our lives, we have the choice to be in the arena or to be a bystander. We can choose to be in the arena, trying new things or we can be a bystander who watches what others do and critiques from afar.

In my youth, I was a state ten-pin bowler with a high score of 299. I trained to read the lane conditions, to strengthen my technique, and to hit the pocket to get a strike as many times as possible during a game. Even though I never bowled a perfect game, I was still a good ten-pin bowler. I had a high average and I spent hours training on spares to maximise my score. I could have saved myself time by not training on spares, by giving up after I didn't get a strike. I trained for Plan B. I trained for the second frame.

Winning as a team or individual felt fantastic. It was electric and satisfying. In contrast, losing didn't feel good. After the competition ended, we would have a debrief with the coach to regroup and reflect on what had happened. There were days when I dreaded the debriefs because I knew my game wasn't good and I felt I had let myself and the team down. I took losing personally because I wanted to perform at my best each time I stepped onto the approach.

Over time, I realised that failure was part of success. I learned more about myself, the team dynamics, and the game when we lost or made mistakes. There were times where I'd walk back after a shot and speak to the coach because I knew exactly what I did wrong and I wanted to know how I could correct it. Rather than getting frustrated and throwing the game, I sought out help, I trained, and I learned. That's when my game began to improve. I didn't strive for perfection. I accepted that I wouldn't always perform at my best. I chose to focus on doing my best on that day. If something about my technique wasn't working, I refrained from getting frustrated and instead I started to look for solutions. What could I change to improve my game? How could I still contribute the highest score to the team? Those were questions I would ask myself and while I didn't always find a way to improve my game, I knew that I had tried. I didn't just give up and accept defeat.

Whether it's on a sports field, an office or in another part of your life, mistakes and failure are not final. If you've failed or made a mistake, it doesn't mean you won't succeed at that thing or succeed at something else. It's all part of the process.

If you have failed at something, it doesn't make you a failure as a person. It took me a long time to disassociate from my failings and to stop saying I was a failure when I failed. It was a default response, a persona I took on. Perhaps it's your persona, too but it doesn't have to be.

Ironically, I never called myself a success when I succeeded at something. It's often easier for us to take on a negative persona than it is a positive one. This isn't surprising when you learn that our brains are hardwired to have a negative bias. This bias kept our ancestors safe from harm, such as poisonous plants which could have killed them. Like anything, too much of a good thing can become a bad thing. For us in the modern world, the negative bias helps us keep score of our mistakes. If you were asked to recall a failure and a success you've had in life, how long would it take you to think of each one? My guess is, you'll be able to list a few failures before you can name a success.

Once we begin to accept that failure is part of success, we can shift our focus. Rather than dwelling on the mistake and being stuck where we are, we can reflect on what happened and move forward. If you find yourself overthinking and feeling like you're a failure, I want you to take a moment and pause. If you have failed at something, it means you have tried something new. That's an achievement within itself because you've dared to try something out of your comfort zone. You've been courageous and stepped inside the arena. For me, failure happens when we don't try anything new at all. It's when we give up before we've even started. The failure or mistake also gives you invaluable information and experience. As Henry Ford said, "you can begin again, this time more wisely."

Imagine if people gave up after their first failed attempt at something new. While I can only speculate, I'm certain that we wouldn't have some of the items and comforts we use today. Whether you're learning a new skill, creating a product, building a business, or inventing something tangible or intangible, chances are you'll make a mistake along the way. That doesn't detract from your success, and it shouldn't be a reason to give up.

When you can learn from the mistakes and failures, you build resilience. You know that you are still capable, irrespective of the outcome. You're not attached to the outcome, rather it's about learning what you can along the way. If you can look at trying new things as a science experiment, each attempt is a new method. Sometimes the method to test the hypothesis works on the first go and other times many attempts are required to reach the specified outcome. Allow yourself the chance to experiment and to learn through trial and error.

One of the great things about making mistakes or failing at something is you don't know what the result could be. We assume that if it's not the result we're expecting that any other result will be bad. When it may be better than what you were thinking or benefit more people. For instance, work policies often arise from a mistake happening. There's a gap in the system, the organisational structure, or the collective or individual knowledge. Without the mistake occurring, there would be no trigger for the policy to be created and implemented. Mistakes can bring clarity on boundaries, standards, and preventative tools for the future to minimise the chance of it happening again.

We could apply a similar thought process to relationships. Would you consider yourself a failure at relationships if you are single or have had a few breakups? I'd hope not. Whether it's a platonic or romantic relationship ending, you are not a failure if it didn't work out the way you had hoped. Reflect on what the relationship gave and taught you and use that to ascertain what you would like in relationships moving forward. Sometimes, the quickest way to work out what you want is by identifying what you don't want.

Individuals who have achieved great levels of success are not immune to making mistakes or failing. The difference is, they don't allow their mistakes to stop them from continuing. They don't allow their goal to be derailed by a mistake. They reflect, pivot, and change their approach. They use the new information to help them make progress. They separate themselves from the situation and identify when something isn't working without thinking they're a failure in the process.

I'd encourage you to reflect on how you respond to mistakes and failure. Do you stop working on your goal when you've made a mistake or failed? Or do you pause, reflect on what caused the mistake, what you learned from it, and then continue?

If you want to achieve your goals, you'll need to be prepared to fail and make mistakes. The bigger the goal, the more likely you are to encounter challenges and roadblocks. It is rare, especially with larger goals for it to be completely smooth sailing. There are usually hiccups along the way and that's all part of the process. If you do feel defeated and want to quit on your goal, that is your prerogative. Take a moment to reflect on why you want to quit and whether it's an impulsive decision. Mistakes and failing doesn't feel pleasant and to avoid the feeling, we may step into protection mode by walking away from the goal. We stop ourselves from feeling disappointed, embarrassed, ashamed or like a failure in the short term. Yet, we may regret that choice later if it wasn't made from the right place.

At thirty, I made the decision to close my candle business. I started the business when I was twenty-seven during the pandemic and after 2.5 years of trying to increase sales, brand awareness, and get into the market scene I decided to call it a day. While it may have seemed like a sudden decision when I announced it on the business social media channels, it was something I had been considering for the previous six months. I tried different things during my final year of business to try and increase sales including pouring my heart into building a website. Then one day I just knew it was time to close. I haven't regretted my decision as I know I made the right choice.

Business isn't easy. It's a steep learning curve and there's so much information on the internet, in books, on podcasts and social media about how to build a brand, increase sales and so forth. At times, it was overwhelming and when I wasn't getting the results I thought I should be getting, I felt like I was failing. I didn't have anyone show up to several of the market stalls I put on which was disheartening. That was what motivated me to try different things in my final year of business and when I saw that wasn't working, I accepted it. I made peace with the decision to close the business and not perceive it as a failure. I learned a lot during the business venture and the fact that I took a chance by starting the business, was enough for me to not consider it a failure.

If writers quit after their first rejection letter, there'd be popular books that no one would have had the opportunity to read and appreciate. If actors quit after their first audition not resulting in a job offer, how many leading men and women would we never see on the big screen? If Thomas Edison stopped attempting to make a light bulb, what would we use for lighting? The list goes on. Whether it's a goal that will change one life or many, you have the option to choose how you deal with and navigate the hardships during the process.

I hope you can find a way to carry on with your goal despite the mistakes along the way. When you look back, you'll likely be able to connect the dots and see why it happened the way it did. Remember, mistakes teach us more than success.

Children have an innate ability to try, fail and try again until they get it right. Granted there may be tears, feelings of frustrating and impatience, but they keep persevering. Failed attempts enable us to build grit and resilience. Failed attempts enable us to walk and tie our shoelaces.

So what happened to that younger version of you who wasn't attached to their failures? Somewhere between childhood and adulthood many of us lost that level of resilience and grit. We learned to fear making mistakes. We created a story around failure. It became something we learned to be ashamed of. We didn't want to feel embarrassed by our performance so we stopped trying altogether. If we weren't good at something we would simply stop trying. By not trying, it gave us a sense of control over the outcome. By not trying, we could guarantee a safe outcome of did not complete. Noone could measure our performance because we chose not to participate. There could be no judgement from others or ourselves.

Failing began to mean we were a failure. To use a sporting analogy, no one makes 100% of the shots they take. When we strive for perfection by never failing, we are telling ourselves that failure is not an option. If we fail, we are not good enough. We want everything to go smoothly all the time. If there's a chance of failure we may not be willing to take the risk. In doing so we stunt our own growth. Remember, failing does not make you a failure. Failing gives you an opportunity to learn.

Until my mid-twenties, I was attached to my failures. I took it personally and created a story in my mind that I am a failure when I fail. I wasn't able or willing to look beyond the perceived failure to realise that to fail at something meant I had given something a go. When I started to read biographies and listen to podcasts about people who were successful in life and their careers, I realised that their paths to success weren't straight forward. In their books, these individuals shared insights into the trials and errors which led them to where they are now. Their willingness to share their story of success was pivotal for my own mindset change. I realised that trying and failing was better than not trying at all. I may not have achieved the result I hoped for, but I still tried. It wasn't the end either. You can fail forwards and learn from the mistake. Often a mistake leads us to where we're meant to be.

If you're applying for a job, you may or may not make it to the interview stage. If you do get an interview, your chances of being offered the role increases. Your interview may go well, or it might not. If you don't get the job offer, it doesn't mean you have failed and are unemployable. You can ask for feedback to see where you can improve for your next interview. The job which is meant for you, will find you.

If you're someone who perceives failure to be a negative, I'd encourage you to change your perspective. I know it doesn't always feel like it but failure is a sign that you are trying. If we didn't make mistakes or fail, how would we grow and expand our skill set? As children, we were resilient. We kept trying to walk, speak, swim, cycle, and tie our shoes until we got it right. We didn't think about how many attempts it would take. We just kept going. We didn't see each failed attempt as the end point, we saw it as an opportunity to try again. It's possible to return to this way of thinking and being.

Perhaps you're wondering how to change your definition of failure and stop embodying it. I am grateful for personal development because it gave me the tools to change my failure narrative and to apply a growth mindset approach, which you can do too.

Learning to detach from a failure isn't an overnight fix. Subconsciously, many of us attach our self-worth to the outcome of a situation. If everything goes well – fantastic! If it doesn't, that's when we start to berate and shame ourselves. For many of us, this process isn't conscious, you may not even know when you started to attach your worth to the outcome. Now that you have this new level of self-awareness you can begin to consciously change your behaviours. It takes time to rewrite the thought process associated with learning and failing.

Throughout my twenties, I have applied for jobs when I've felt ready to move on from my current employer. At twenty-three, I desperately wanted to resign from the travel agent role I was in because the company values didn't resonate with me. I was applying for many jobs, and I took each rejection to heart. I spent hours on finessing one job application package and when I received the rejection, I cried. I felt like giving up. After a conversation with Jesse, I was able to view it from a different perspective and I began to not take the rejections personally. From that point onwards, I have learned to trust that I will find the right job. If a job application is rejected, it's because that wasn't the right job for me. I'll share the process I used to change my relationship with failure.

Instead of feeling ashamed and embarrassed when I failed, I decided to shift my focus. I was focusing on the outcome and attaching my worth to how the outcome unfolded. If the outcome didn't go as I anticipated it, I would define it as a failure. There were times when the outcome was better than I had expected but for the most part I was focused on whether there was a failure or not. If I failed, I would dwell on it and feel ashamed. I'd stew in these feelings until something snapped me out of it.

If the result was as expected my old thought pattern was one of relief. I had avoided an embarrassing, shameful failure. If the result was not as expected I would take it personally and feel like a failure as a person. I'd feel stuck, embarrassed, and ashamed. I wouldn't look for any lessons that might be learned. I wasn't grateful and I wasn't willing to reflect on why I got that result.

Once I had self-development tools and understood more about the principles of having a growth mindset, I decided to shift my perspective and focus on my input instead. Generally, I was able to control how much effort I put into the situation. I began to detach from the outcome and if I knew I gave 100% that was enough regardless of the outcome. If the outcome could have been better, I'd get curious about how I could improve.

Now if the result was good or better than I had expected my new thought pattern was one of gratitude. If the results wasn't what I had hoped I looked for lessons and learned from the situation. I chose to perceive it as an opportunity for learning and growth rather than believing I'm a failure because it didn't work out as I had expected. I was grateful for trying and for the new information I received from the experience.

I began to focus on the lessons to be learned rather than outcome. I no longer allowed my failed attempts to define me. Instead I was able to feel gratitude for the failure as it meant I was going to learn something new. There's never one outcome or one way to do something so if you don't reach the outcome on the first try, it just means there's another way.

Affirmations:

1. I am learning as I work towards my goals.
2. I try and succeed. I try and fail. Both are parts of my journey to success.
3. I learn from my mistakes.
4. I am open to trying new things.
5. If something doesn't work, I try something new.

Journal prompts:

1. What does the word failure mean to me?
2. Do I allow my failures to define me?
3. Is the word 'failure' negatively or positively charged?
4. When I fail, how does that make me feel? Both emotionally and physically.
5. Am I open to redefining my definition of failure? If so, what is my

new definition?

6. Do I associate failure with success?
7. What is my definition of success?
8. How does a person I admire handle failure? What can I take away from their approach?

Activity:

Depending on your answers to the above journal prompts, you may want to complete one or both of the following activities:

1. Reflect on a time when you have failed and how you handled the situation; or
2. Research a person you admire and how they deal with failure.

The purpose of this activity is to help you look at failure from a different perspective. While a core belief cannot be changed overnight, it is possible to change it gradually. If you are open to changing your perception of success and believing it is part of your path to success, then this activity will help you do so.

Lesson Ten: When You're Lacking Motivation, Try Discipline.

Don't expect to be motivated everyday to get out there and make things happen. You won't be. Don't count on motivation. Count on discipline. - Jocko.

During my time at university, I remember thinking how cool it would be if you could bottle motivation and take a shot of it when needed. Ironically, I didn't have the motivation to put any further thought into that idea.

Motivation can be defined as a driving force which encourages you to take action or engage in goal orientated behaviours. You don't need to be motivated to start, yet many of us won't act until we are motivated.

Motivation or the lack thereof becomes a valid reason for why we aren't doing things. "I'm just not feeling it (motivated) today," we say. As a result of not feeling motivated, we don't take action. I'll let you in on a little secret. If I had waited to feel motivated to write this book, you wouldn't be holding it in your hands. Motivation is a nice feeling but it's fleeting and sometimes we just need to get started irrespective of whether we feel motivated or not.

We've all had days where we haven't felt motivated to complete a task. We just feel average. Whether it's procrastinating on an assignment, a work task, or personal goal it's time to stop letting ourselves off the hook when we're lacking motivation. But how can we do that exactly?

For most of my twenties, I had these two beliefs about motivation and taking action. I would wait to feel motivated and if the motivation didn't come, I wouldn't take action. Or I would wait to feel motivated and if the motivation did come, I would take action. This limited my productivity because I was waiting for a feeling which seldom came. I wouldn't act if I didn't feel motivated. I'd wait until I felt motivated to act. Motivation or the lack thereof was my excuse for why I had or hadn't done something. I spent more time justifying why I hadn't started or completed something than I did working on it.

If you also find yourself waiting for motivation before working on a task, I encourage you to reflect on the following questions.

- Do I wait to feel motivated before I start working on a task?
- What does feeling motivated look like?
- Why do I wait to feel motivated?
- Does motivation come? If not, what do I do?
- What's the result of this process?
- What is inaction costing me?
- Am I open to taking action before I feel motivated?

When I reflected on these questions, I came to discover that the result of me waiting for motivation was inconsistency, inaction, and a belief of, "If I'm not motivated, I won't take action." This reflection happened when I was twenty-five. I was trying to implement a new morning routine and I noticed that I wasn't consistent with it. I was disciplined enough to set an alarm however, if I work up feeling tired or unmotivated, I would stay in bed. I was letting myself off the hook constantly and then feeling guilty for not completing the morning routine. I knew I felt better once I had completed the new routine yet that wasn't enough to motivate me. I get fed up with my own inaction and decided to stop waiting to feel motivated. After this reflection, I decided to change my approach. I set my alarm, got up and completed the routine. I didn't give myself a chance to ask if I felt motivated that morning and I began to rely on discipline. Instead of waiting to feel motivated, I chose to take action first. If motivation was a bi-product then great. If it wasn't I learned to believe that I was disciplined enough to keep going. Simply put, I took action rather than waiting for a certain feeling.

I wish I could give you a magic wand that made you feel motivated every time you were about to take action but I can't. Motivation doesn't work with wave of a magic wand. If we can't rely on motivation, what can we do instead?

We can learn to become disciplined. If you want to get to a place where you take consistent action, discipline will help you get there.

According to Collins Dictionary, discipline is defined as "the ability to behave and work in a controlled way which involves obeying particular rules or standards." If we go one step further, Collins Dictionary defines self-discipline as "the ability to control yourself and to make yourself work hard or behave in a particular way without needing anyone else to tell you what to do."

The greater your level of self-discipline, the greater your chance of achieving results. Self-disciplined individuals are self-starters and can work in autonomous environments because they don't rely on motivation or others to get started. Instead, they rely on their patterns of behaviours such as routines and habits to support them in taking action.

Discipline may be a virtue, but it is also a learned skill. If you want to become more self-disciplined, it is possible. Here are a few strategies you can implement cultivate self-discipline:

- Limit distractions. When you're setting aside time to work on your goal, don't be afraid to put your phone on do not disturb and block out time in your calendar. When you limit your distractions you'll be less tempted to mindlessly scroll as a way of procrastinating.

- Learn about your strengths and weaknesses in relation to your goal. What do you need to strengthen or overcome to achieve your goal? Can you outsource parts of your goal or learn more about it?
- Honour the commitments you make with yourself. If you wouldn't cancel on a loved one, why would you cancel on yourself? If you set aside time to work on your goal, honour it. Once you begin to honour your commitments more and more, it will become second nature.
- Have a clear plan of what you want to achieve. Clarity yields results. Set a goal and work towards it. If the goal seems too large break it down into smaller pieces and work through it gradually.
- Get started whether you're feeling motivated or not by telling yourself you only have to do the task for 10 minutes.
- Be realistic. This may sound contradictory, but you may not always be able to follow your daily habits and routine perfectly every day. Life happens and if you miss a milestone or break a habit streak, accept it and try again the next day or time you've allocated to it.

I created discipline around writing this book. I implemented several strategies to help me stay focused and make progress. The strategies included: setting aside time to work on the book without distractions for a minimum amount of time, writing my book electronically so I could work on it while I was travelling and sharing information about my progress on social media. I would sit outside in our backyard with my laptop and a cup of cacao for a minimum of 30 minutes. If I set aside writing time on a weekend, I would often write for an hour. I knew this was the maximum amount of time I could write without feeling the need to look for a distraction – such as my phone. By working outside, I was able to limit distractions by leaving my phone inside. I chose to write this book electronically rather than by hand because I had a few trips planned and I wanted it to be portable. Instead of watching movies on flights, I opted to pull out my laptop and make progress on my book. These were some of my best writing sessions because my mind was clear and I didn't have any distractions. Lastly, I shared my progress on social media. By sharing my goal, it helped me stay accountable to making progress because friends and family would ask how the manuscript was progressing.

If you wait to feel motivated before starting on a task, try focus on building discipline instead. You won't feel motivated everyday but that's not a reason to not continue working on your goals, projects and bettering yourself. By reflecting on the questions in the chapter, using the affirmations and journal prompts below, you can begin to focus on the areas of your life where you can build discipline.

Affirmations:

1. I honour the commitments I make to myself and others.
2. I am committed to working towards my goals.
3. I choose discipline over motivation.
4. I use my time wisely.
5. I am an action taker.

Journal prompts:

1. In what areas of my life would I like to be more disciplined?
2. If I catch myself waiting to feel motivated before I act, what will I do instead?
3. Am I willing to take action when I don't feel motivated?
4. Am I willing to accept that I won't always feel motivated?

Activity:

It's time to start working on a task that you've been putting off until you had the motivation to do it. If it's a larger task, feel free to break it down into smaller tasks and complete one.

Once you've completed it, reflect on how you felt before, during and after you completed it. Did you feel motivated to start? If you didn't, were you tempted to put the task off? How did you feel during the task? Did you begin to feel motivated? If you didn't, did you have a mindset shift? Lastly, how did you feel once you completed it?

Lesson Eleven: When You Have Boundaries And Standards.

You get what you tolerate. - Henry Cloud.

The notion of personal boundaries gained traction in the 1980s. While there are varying definitions of what a personal boundary entails, this definition encapsulates the concept succinctly. A boundary is "the limit you set for yourself that defines what you are willing to do, accept or tolerate. It protects your right to have your own thoughts and feelings and guards them from being criticized or invalidated."

Boundaries are the metaphorical lines in the sand that each of us draws. Boundaries are not the same as putting up walls to keep people from getting to you or getting to know you. The purpose of a boundary is to inform others of what actions, words, and behaviours you're willing to tolerate and those you aren't. The type of personal boundaries you can set include but aren't limited to: physical, emotional, time, work, verbal and financial.

Boundaries can be rigid or flexible. You may wish or need to draw a hard line with certain boundaries, yet with others you may be more flexible. A rigid boundary could be not engaging with anyone who is yelling at you. Rather than continue the conversation you could advise the person that you do not engage with people who are yelling and walk away. A flexible boundary could be your work schedule. You may have standard days and hours to work each week. There may be occasions where you need to change your schedule and this would be the exception, rather than the rule.

It is an act of self-love and respect to have boundaries in place which serve you. It may feel selfish, especially if you feel resistance from others but it is for you to decide what you will and won't tolerate. Your boundaries are in place to honour your needs and when this is communicated effectively with others, they will know what behaviour you will and won't tolerate. If they choose to overstep a boundary that is their decision. If you have communicated your boundary effectively then others can choose to respect it or deal with the consequences of overstepping it.

Throughout my twenties I struggled with creating, setting, and maintaining boundaries. It felt uncomfortable to me. I was okay with how things were and didn't want to disrupt the status quo in my relationships. I would rather be frustrated by things than create or communicate a boundary. My primary focus was on how others would perceive me. I didn't want to be perceived as a bitch.

After some internal reflection after attending a self-care workshop at twenty-eight, I realised I had created a story around boundaries. The workshop included a session on boundaries and on the drive home, I reflected on mine. I reflected on the boundaries I didn't have in place but wanted to and what was stopping me from implementing them. I realised the story I held around boundaries needed to change. I thought someone with boundaries would be perceived negatively. However, I perceive people with boundaries as being self-assured, respectable, and empowered. Once I identified how I perceived others who had boundaries I was more open to setting boundaries. After my realisation and reflection, I wrote down a list of boundaries I wanted to implement, and I set about doing so. Boundaries allow you to protect your energy, time, and money. I'd be creating them for me, not for others.

Others may not appreciate or respect your boundaries and that is their choice to make, just as it is yours to create one in the first place. If you haven't set many boundaries it may come as shock to those around you when you start to assert yourself and communicate what you will and won't tolerate. A lack of boundaries serves others and it's time to put yourself first.

Jesse and I enjoy hosting dinners with friends and family. I believe that arriving 15-30 minutes before the communicated start time is just as, if not more impolite than being late. I feel that if a start time has been given it is polite to arrive at or after that time, not before. On several occasions we had guests arrive before the start time, begin eating the food, and wanting to have a conversation while we were still getting ready. It put me in a bad mood and I felt stressed. I kept my thoughts to myself and chose to let the behaviour slide. I tolerated this behaviour because I didn't want to seem impolite. After all, we did offer to have people over for dinner. A few years passed and it happened again. This time rather than let the people into the house and tolerate the behaviour, I had a conversation with them which went along the lines of… "Hey, thanks so much for being here. It's still thirty minutes before the event starts and we're busy preparing the food. We aren't ready to start hosting yet, would you mind visiting people nearby and coming back at the start time?" They seemed surprised I had asked, yet they respected my request and came back later. Since that conversation they have arrived on time or after. In the moment it felt incredibly uncomfortable to communicate my needs, but I also felt a huge wave of stress pass over me when I heard them arriving. I knew I'd feel more uncomfortable letting them in and not owning my needs than I would if I asked them to come back later.

It may feel uncomfortable to communicate your boundary with others. However, an uncommunicated boundary often leads to resentment and frustration because others aren't aware of your silent want or need. They aren't aware that they're overstepping an invisible boundary and it's unreasonable for us to expect others to be mind readers. There have been times when I've unknowingly overstepped someone's boundary and I was relieved when they communicated that with me.

In a former workplace my colleagues and I were chatting about life outside of work. We were all having a good laugh and sharing information. We were on the topic of birthdays and I asked one of my colleagues when their birthday was. The response I got was a short, "That's none of your business." I felt taken aback by the response because I didn't think it was impolite to ask, especially when we were all sharing. Later my colleague explained that they didn't like to talk about their birth date for personal reasons. By sharing this information with me I knew not to talk about birthdays with this person moving forward. I respected their feelings on the topic. Sometimes, we don't know that we've overstepped. Once something has been brought to our attention you'll need to decide whether you're going to respect the boundary or overstep it.

I believe people don't intend to cause stress or harm. If they're unaware there's an issue they don't have the opportunity to reflect and potentially change their behaviour in the future.

Boundaries are essential to your health and well-being. I'd encourage you to reflect on what feelings come up for you when you hear the word boundaries. Does it make you feel good, or do you feel yourself tensing up? Do you feel like you have good boundaries in place or are they something you're wanting to implement?

Boundaries can be perceived as positive or negative depending on the situation. If you're new to setting boundaries, it may feel awkward and difficult. You may receive pushback from others who are impacted by your new boundaries. This could be because of a resistance to change or because the absence of that boundary was beneficial for them.

With a boundary in place they stand to lose something. For instance, if you have a small business and your customers are accustomed to being able to message you at all hours and get an instant response, some may be taken aback if you implemented a new boundary around when you'll reply to messages. Alternatively, say you're wanting to create a boundary around what topics you will and won't discuss with certain people. It may feel uncomfortable having the conversation and explaining what topics you won't be open to discussing moving forward. However, the longer you delay implementing the boundary the more it will impact you.

A boundary is a limit or space you put between yourself and someone else. It helps others know what you're willing to tolerate, do, or accept. Personal boundaries can include physical, emotional, mental, financial, time, and intellectual. This is not an exhaustive list and given that personal boundaries are exactly that…personal, you can choose what you want to set a boundary around.

As each of us has different wants and needs our boundaries will be different. Therefore, trying to define what makes a good boundary is near impossible due to the subjective nature of them. When I've successfully set and implemented a boundary it feels freeing because I've communicated with others what I will and won't accept. Whether they choose to accept and embrace my boundary is then up to them. We can't control if people respect our boundary or not but that shouldn't stop you from creating one.

There may be different ways you can communicate your boundary depending on who the boundary will affect and how. If the boundary is around a behaviour you could wait for the behaviour to occur again to communicate your new boundary or you could advise the person before the behaviour occurs again.

Let's say you have a friend who is never ready when you offer to pick them up for an event and you want to set a boundary around how long you'll wait. You could:

1. Wait until you're collecting them for an event and when they're ready late you could say, "Hey. I value my time and yours so moving forward can you please be ready on time when I pick you up? In the future if you are running late and don't let me know, I'll wait for five minutes before heading off."
2. When you next catch up you could bring up the boundary in the conversation. "Hey. The event we went to recently was fun. I'm happy to pick you up on a way to an event but when you're running late I get stressed out because I want us to be on time. Moving forward can you please be ready on time? If you don't let me know in advance, I'll wait five minutes before driving off."

In both examples you have clearly articulated what your boundary is and the consequence if the boundary isn't followed without belittling your friend. You've focused on how the situation makes you feel, the behaviour that causes it, and what you'll do if the behaviour continues. You haven't made it about your friend, you've just explained how it makes you feel, and what you'll do next time.

Now that you've created and implemented your boundary, you'll need to be consistent. People may resist your boundaries or try to test how strongly you hold them. It is up to you how flexible or firm you'd like to be with your boundaries. There may be times when you are willing to compromise and bend a boundary. If I'm unsure whether I want to be flexible with a boundary or to stay firm with enforcing it I'll ask myself, "Who will it benefit?" If the other person is the only person who wins from you not enforcing a boundary, it may be worth standing firm. If you both gain something from the flexibility, then it's up to you whether you choose to bend.

Continuing from the example above, if your friend is running late for the next event after you've had the conversation about your boundary, you have a choice to make. Do you drive away after five minutes (as you explained in your conversation) or wait longer (be flexible with your boundary)? If you are not used to having boundaries executing the consequence may feel mean, harsh, and uncomfortable. The boundary is there to serve you. You've communicated with the person what behaviour you will and won't tolerate. You'll need to decide which discomfort bothers you more, the discomfort of running late for another event or the discomfort of driving off after five minutes of waiting.

What if your friend is running ten minutes late but they've let you know with plenty of time. You could still drive off after five minutes, or you could compromise and wait longer because they let you know which shows they're valuing your time. There's no right or wrong answer but it's something you'll need to consider. It's an opportunity for you empower yourself to make a decision that prioritises your well-being rather than one that compromises it If you continue to wait for your friend without setting a boundary around how long you'll wait for them before leaving, your stress and discomfort levels will increase. You'll continue to put yourself in a stressful situation because your friend doesn't know how you feel about their tardiness. If you create a boundary, your stress levels will reduce because your friend knows the consequences of crossing the boundary. They now know how you feel about their tardiness and you have an option for handling the situation differently. You will no longer need to wait around or be rushing to get to the destination. There isn't a right or wrong answer with strict or flexible boundaries either. It's all about providing a way for you to be respected while maintaining open and honest communication.

What happens if a person doesn't accept your boundary? If you've communicated your boundary and the consequences if it isn't adhered to, it's up to that person to accept or reject it. If someone rejects your boundary, it's their choice. You cannot force someone to adhere to, accept, or respect your boundary. The boundaries I've been scared to implement are the ones which I need to the most or the ones I am expecting pushback on. If you haven't had many boundaries before, it may come as a surprise to people, especially those who benefitted from your lack of boundaries.

You will likely find that your boundaries will change and evolve as you move through different periods in your life. In my early twenties, I didn't have many boundaries, especially around my availability. I tried to be easy-going and spontaneous. I wanted to be perceived as carefree and easy going. In my late twenties, I started to create boundaries around my time. As the amount of free time I had decreased, I would say no to events which were organised last minute. I may not have had another event to go to however, I had already allocated that time to working on a goal, spending time with Jesse or doing something around the house and I was no longer prepared to drop what I was doing to accommodate someone else's last-minute plans. In my thirties, I have created boundaries around topics I will or won't discuss with others. As Jesse and I enter parenthood, my/our boundaries will evolve again. If you reflect on boundaries you've created over the years, you'll notice the evolution of them. Boundaries don't need to last forever and they can change as you move through life. Some boundaries may be temporary and others may last for a longer period of time depending on what it is.

Once you begin to create, communicate, and implement boundaries, it'll get easier with time. What feels daunting to do can sometimes be the best thing for you. You'll be glad once you've started, I promise.

To paraphrase Thomas Leonard, boundaries are what you have determined others or an environment cannot do to you. Boundaries allow you to say no. On the other hand, standards refer to the behaviours and levels of excellence you hold yourself to. Standards allow you to say yes to yourself. I believe there is a relationship between boundaries, standards, and self-worth. Someone with low self-worth will likely have fewer boundaries and lower standards compared to someone who is confident and self-assured. You don't need to wait until you've reached a certain level of confidence to set boundaries and create standards for yourself. You can begin today. As a flow on effect, you can increase your standards and levels of self-worth in the process. You may hold yourself to a high standard or have lower standards all in different areas of your life. If you want to lower or raise the standard you set and expect from yourself there is nothing stopping you.

You're allowed to want more for and from yourself. This is where creating standards can be helpful. Whether it's a standard around your work ethic, workout routine, having a hobby, or how you take care of yourself. You get to set the standard. When you begin to set standards for yourself, this will likely be noticed by others and they may choose to raise their own standards or maintain their own more consistently. Just remember, it's easier to focus on your own standards than it is trying to get others to change theirs.

Around the age of twenty-seven I got into the habit of wearing activewear to shopping centres. There would be times when I'd go to the shops after a walk or hike but other times I would choose to wear activewear for a specific trip. While there's nothing wrong with wearing activewear around the place, I wanted to raise the standard for myself. I wanted to revert to wearing non-activewear clothing. I decided to set a new standard. I would cease wearing activewear to the shops. The exception to the rule would be if I was going to the shops immediately following a fitness activity. Since I implemented this standard, I've adhered to it. I feel better when I'm at the shops in a casual outfit of jeans and a top compared to activewear.

While this standard may seem silly or insignificant to some, for me it made a difference. Standards are personal and their purpose is to help you say yes to yourself and express yourself the way you want to. Standards are not permanent and they can be changed, removed, or improved over time. You are the maker of your standards. What you focus on is up to you.

If you are wanting to create new standards of behaviour for yourself, I recommend thinking it through using the following process to set yourself up for success.

1. Identify the standard of behaviour you'd like to have and why. It's important to be clear on why the standard is important to you as there may be moments when you're tempted to lower the standard.
2. What is your current standard for this area of your life? What will need to change to reach the new standard? (This will identify the gap between where you are currently and where you want to be. Think of what needs to change or be implemented).
3. Is there something you need to give up or stop doing to allow you to reach and maintain this new standard? It could be a habit, routine, or thought pattern.
4. What will you need to start doing to reach and maintain this new standard? Do you need an accountability partner, to track your progress, or make space in your schedule for it?

Now let's begin! Track your progress and be kind to yourself. It will take time to reach and maintain the new standard. An old habit needs to be break and a new one created.

In my early twenties I strived to be a low maintenance person. I thought being high maintenance was something to be avoided and an unlikeable trait in a person. After watching romantic comedies where the female leads were too much and hearing some of my guy friends talk about not wanting to date high maintenance women, I vowed to be low maintenance. I didn't want a remark such as "Oh, that person is such high maintenance!" to be directed at me, ever. Perhaps you've said or heard this remark at some point throughout your life.

If someone has high standards, does that make them high maintenance? Possibly, but is being high maintenance really a bad thing? If someone is "high maintenance", wouldn't it mean that they've simply communicated their boundaries and standards? The thing about boundaries and standards is that it causes someone to re-evaluate how they are behaving. If they need to change their behaviour, it may be easier to deflect responsibility by saying someone is just being high maintenance rather than taking responsibility for their behaviour.

Upon reflection later in my twenties, I realised that I would rather be perceived as high maintenance than allow others to walk all over me. I'd rather communicate my boundaries and create standards of behaviour that I'd like to adhere to over going with the flow to my own detriment.

I've chosen to change my definition of high maintenance to, 'a high maintenance individual is a person who has strong boundaries, clearly defined standards, is someone who knows their purpose, and leads by example.' This definition represents an individual who is self-aware, self-confident, and not egotistical. It now feels like a positive trait rather than a negative one.

I now consider a low maintenance person to be someone who goes with the flow, has minimal boundaries, and tries not to impose on others. A low maintenance person may be perceived by others as agreeable and personable because they are happy to adapt to the needs and opinions of others, yet there's a downside. I'd suggest that at the cost of being agreeable we are likely to compromise our own boundaries, standards, or opinions.

While my new definition of high maintenance and low maintenance may challenge you, I hope it also encourages you to look at the definitions you have given these terms.

To summarise, standards are for us and boundaries are for others. Sometimes, we have the same expectations of ourselves and others, sometimes we don't. For instance, you may choose to not swear at work (your standard) but it may not bother you if others swear around you at work (boundary).

With the information shared in this lesson, you can begin to create boundaries which allow you to prioritise your own needs, standards that help you become the version of yourself that you're striving to be. With time, you will begin to see the results when you uphold your boundaries and standards.

Affirmations:

1. I am creating boundaries which allow me to focus on my priorities.
2. I allow my boundaries to evolve with me.
3. I have boundaries as an act of self-love and self-respect.
4. I set the standards I expect from myself.
5. I communicate my needs openly with others.

Journal Prompts:

1. What boundary am I struggling to set and why?
2. Who do I know that has strong boundaries? How do I feel about this person/people?
3. Who do I know that has weak boundaries? How do I feel about this person/people?
4. Am I content with the standards I have set for myself?
5. What words and behaviours do I associate with being low maintenance?

6. What words and behaviours do I associate with being high maintenance?

Activity:

Write down a boundary you want to set. List how the boundary will benefit you (time wise, financial, mentally, etc) and how you will communicate it to others. Consider what the consequence will be if someone oversteps the boundary. Next, begin to communicate the boundary with the people who need to be aware of it. If feelings come up or you experience resistance from others, journal and reflect on it. Decide whether you'll stand firm with your boundary or if it may need to be revised.

How do you create and implement a boundary? If it's an overdue boundary that you're trying to implement, I'd encourage you to sit down and think about the following:

1. What is the purpose of the boundary?
2. Who will the boundary affect?
3. How will you advise the affected party/ies of your new boundary?
4. Are you comfortable enforcing your boundary?
5. How do you feel without the boundary / how do you want to feel once it's implemented?

Asking yourself these questions when you're ready to create a boundary will help you implement it confidently. When you know the purpose, who will be affected, how you'll communicate it, how you want to feel once the boundary is in effect and how you'll enforce it if others try to overstep, you'll be more likely to maintain it.

Lesson Twelve: When You Realise Personal Development Is A Lifelong Journey.

Personal growth is a journey, not a destination. Embrace the process, celebrate your progress and trust in the magic of your potential. - Unknown.

Personal development is a journey, not a destination. You can continue to grow and evolve throughout your life, if you choose. Once you gain the awareness of personal development and how it can impact your life it becomes a way of life. To paraphrase the Cambridge English Dictionary, personal development consists of activities that develops one's capabilities and potential, enhances quality of life and facilitates the realisation of dreams and aspirations. It's gaining awareness and an understanding your beliefs, thoughts, emotions and how they influence your behaviour, choices and how you live your life. This level of understanding cannot be achieved overnight. It is something that is worked on for an undefined amount of time. The length of time and depth of the experience varies from person to person.

At the beginning of my journey, I had moments where I thought personal development was a fleeting notion. That I could read about the topic, make a few tweaks to my life and bam, I'd be a completely different person with a new lifestyle. I thought personal development offered a series of quick fixes and once implemented, I could call it day. Now I believe it to be a journey. For some, that journey may last several years and for others, a lifetime.

Let me take you back to when I was twenty-four. Jesse and I were getting ready to host our first family Christmas at his house and I wanted to be organised. During a lunch break at work I was wandering around the city and found a store called Kikki K. On the window were dates for an upcoming Christmas workshop. I entered the store in to enquire about the workshop. I walked out with a booking confirmation and a book called *Thrive* by Arianna Huffington.

That book changed the trajectory of my life. I understand that is a huge statement to make but it truly did. That book ignited something in me which I never knew existed. Perhaps it was always there, and the book was just the ignition. In the book I found a subject which not only fascinated me, but also felt so familiar. It felt like a homecoming in a way because as a kid I was drawn to quotes and song lyrics. I was moved by words. There were times when I would read a quote or listen to a song and it reminded me that I wasn't the only person who had experienced that thing.

The notion of personal development captivated me. I liked the idea that we weren't set in our ways. We could learn new ways of doing and being, if we were open to it. We could create a self-care toolkit that helps us navigate the highs and lows of life. It brought so many of the quotes I once had hanging on my bedroom wall to life. They weren't just words anymore. They were concepts I could learn and implement.

After I finished reading the book, I knew I was ready to make changes to myself and in my life. I wanted to learn more about the different aspects of personal development. I wanted to become more aware of who I was and why I did the things I did. I began to feel empowered to make my own decisions and consciously think about what I wanted in life. I began to think about goals, my purpose, and the woman I wanted to become. I discovered new hobbies. I uncovered and redefined limiting beliefs. And I found yoga, meditation, and other practices which helped me reconnect with myself. This period also brought to life my desire to become an author. Before that it was just a dream.

I was in the Learning Stage of my journey attending events, listening to podcasts and reading books. After a while, I moved into the Experimentation Stage. With all the information I had gathered I felt ready to put what I learned into action. I began to implement the information I was learning from the books and make changes in my life. I'd make a change and evaluate its effectiveness to see if it was something I wanted to commit to long term. I was trying new routines, new habits, and becoming aware of my thoughts and emotions in a deeper way. I became more connected to myself and started to reflect on where I was and where I wanted to be.

The Christmas event that Jesse and I hosted was stressful but successful based on feedback from our guests. I was relieved when the dinner was over, and the guests had left because it meant no more planning, cleaning, cooking or socialising was needed. I learned that if we hosted a Christmas event again, I'd accept the offers from guests to bring a plate of food along because it would make it less stressful having to prepare majority of the food myself. The stress was self-inflicted and if I wasn't being stubborn and accepted their offers, I would have been able to enjoy the event more than I did.

While no journey is identical, I do believe there is a path we tend to follow. The first stage is awareness. As I've shared, I still clearly recall when I first became aware of personal development when I read *Thrive*. It was as if a curtain lifted and I could see a completely new place. I became aware of myself on a different level and realised I could change the direction of my life.

During the Awareness Stage, it can also feel as though the rug has been pulled out from under you. You discover a new way of living and you may realise how long you've been walking through life with a limited sense of direction and limited knowledge of how to make and deal with changes. The awareness is both external and internal. You start to become aware of your habits, characteristics, beliefs, and ideologies. It can be daunting to be confronted with who you are and how you came to be you. Once we become aware of something, we can't unsee it. Equally, it is a beautiful opportunity for growth and personal evolution.

This leads us into the next stage, the Learning Stage. During this stage, you may look inward to learn more about yourself and you may immerse yourself in the works of others. These works may include books, workshops, coaching courses, podcasts, and networking. In the Learning Stage you begin to learn more about concepts you might want to implement into your life. The length of the Learning Stage will vary from person to person. Some prefer to collect information for a longer time while others may get started with the next stage almost immediately.

The next stage is experimentation. Once you have gathered your information, it is time to implement what you have learned, and experiment with how it impacts your life. This stage presents its own challenges as introducing new things into our life requires grit, resilience, and perseverance. It isn't easy to change beliefs, habits, and actions you may have held for decades. It takes practice and time.

The Experimentation Stage gives you the chance to do just that... experiment. You can test out different things to see what works and what doesn't. You can return to the Learning Stage to gather more information too. It may feel like you're back-tracking, but I can assure you, you're not. It takes time, patience, and persistence to build your toolkit.

The final stage is evaluation. In this stage, you can collect data and make observations about what is and isn't working. Try to suspend judgement if something hasn't worked out as you expected. You've tried something new and that's progress in itself. Now you know what doesn't work for you. You may want to ask yourself, "What part of this has or hasn't worked as expected? What can I try instead?"

Now that you have a basic understanding of the different stages, I encourage you to keep moving. This personal development journey is not linear and you will likely find yourself jumping between these stages. Like any method, it has its limitations as it aims to simplify a complex subject.

There will be times throughout your personal development journey when you need to return to the Awareness Stage. Returning to this stage is normal. Throughout our lives we experience different things and it is through these experiences that we learn and discover more about ourselves. I find myself returning to the Awareness Stage when I'm discovering something new about myself. For instance, when I worked with a money coach, I returned to this Stage because prior to that, I didn't pay much attention to my money mindset. I realised it was a part of my mindset I could improve and once I become aware of that, I moved into the Learning Stage.

When I first began to return to the Awareness Stage, I felt like I was taking a step backwards. I thought I wasn't making progress. You may feel that way, too and I want to remind you that you are making progress. Returning to the Awareness Stage shows that you're increasing your awareness of yourself and are open to learning and growing in more aspects of your life. Piece by piece, you are starting to become more aware of your mindset, navigating new experiences and expanding your comfort zone.

You may feel comfortable in the Learning Stage and resist moving into the Experimentation Stage, but if you do not take action you won't see the positive changes that are possible for you. It's like owning a boat and having it docked all the time. The boat does need to be docked at times but that isn't what it was built for.

I was guilty of getting stuck in the information gathering stage. I learned that it is good to consume information but also to know when it is time to implement it. There's no point in collecting information and doing nothing with it. If you're in the Learning Stage, I encourage you to start making minor changes simultaneously.

When I started my online network marketing business, I jumped on the training calls and signed up to a course. I focused on collecting information without bothering to implement it. I rationalised my inaction by telling myself, "I am new to this. I need to know more before I reach out and attempt to build my business." Upon reflection, I realised that I was scared of failure. It was easier to not reach out to potential customers than it was to reach out and hear no. I wanted to know how to be successful in the industry so I invested time and money into courses to help me. I would then think, "I can't spend time working in my business because I'm too busy working on it and learning information." No wonder my business didn't grow.

One of the great things about personal development is that there are a seemingly infinite number of strategies, tools, and activities you can experiment with. There isn't a one size fits all approach. You have the freedom and flexibility to determine what does and doesn't work for you. Not everything you try will be something you'll need to continue doing on a permanent basis either. During stressful times you may implement a daily mindfulness practice such as breathwork, yoga, meditation, or journaling to help you decompress and become grounded. During calmer periods in your life you may use these practices less frequently. They're always there for you to return to.

Early on in my journey I attempted to maintain a daily meditation practice. I'd listen to guided meditations to bring attention to my thoughts and learn how to let them go without getting attached. I found it difficult to clear and calm my mind, and not become attached to thoughts as they entered my head. After a while I realised that meditation was not something I wanted to continue using in my daily routine. In the weeks leading up to this realisation I had been reducing the time I spent listening to a guided meditation each day. Some days I'd try to find a one-minute meditation and other days I'd set aside just five minutes. Or I would play a longer guided mediation but skip a few minutes and still claim that I had meditated that day. Listening to guided meditations was something I wanted to embrace, but I couldn't. Does it mean that I failed? No. I had experimented and found that it didn't work for me. I decided to look for other ways to practice mindfulness. I found yoga and journaling. I noticed that I found stillness in going for walks, soaking up nature, and being in the present moment. To this day a walking mediation when my head is swirling with thoughts is what helps me to clear my mind better than any other mindfulness practice.

I hope you can find your version of a walking meditation. Don't be afraid to experiment with different things on your journey. If something doesn't work for you, try not to become disheartened by it. Accept that you've tried it, make notes from the experiment, and move on to something else. There are many different practices, habits, routines, and skills you can add to your personal development toolkit. It's allowed to look different to everyone else's. It's your toolkit. Fill it with the things that enable you to take care of yourself.

Personal development is a process and an evolution. If you are hoping that personal development tools and frameworks will allow you to change your life overnight, you'll be disappointed. As I mentioned earlier, it isn't a quick fix. Depending on your starting point you could see results quickly. Over time the percentage change in your life will get smaller with each result as you're making more micro changes. Personal development will give you tools to become more self-aware and empower you to learn more about your triggers, beliefs, purpose, and so much more but it isn't a magic wand. If you want to create sustainable change, you'll need to be patient both with yourself and the things you're implementing.

If you're beginning your journey, enjoy it. Take it all in and know that you can make gradual changes along the way. You can experiment, evaluate, and go from there. If something doesn't work, you can stop. You get to choose how your journey unfolds.

Early in my journey I began to unpack and question my deeply held beliefs. I wanted desperately to find my purpose. I became obsessed with trying to determine what my life's purpose was. I was annoyed that other people seemed to know what they wanted to do with their life, while I felt like I had no clue. With hindsight I can laugh about it. At the time it weighed heavily on me that at twenty-three I didn't know what I wanted to do with my life. I felt like I had to decide right now what my life would look like, the impact I wanted to have on the world, and what the purpose of me being here was. I couldn't answer these questions, and I became hyper fixated.

A word of caution. Try not to put too much pressure on yourself to have all the answers. Many self-help books are written by people who are reflecting on their journey so far and they are likely further ahead than you. That's why you're reading their book. That have experienced something you want to learn from. Use their stories, strategies, and tips for guidance and inspiration but don't feel like you should be where they are. As easy as it is for us to fall into the comparison trap, it's not a competition.

With my newfound obsession and passion for personal development, I wanted to change everything immediately. That wasn't practical or sustainable. I was trying to do or change everything at once. Things weren't sticking and I began to feel overwhelmed. Eventually I took a step back and focused on implementing one change at a time. Not only did it become easier to monitor the impacts and results of the changes in my life, it took the pressure off trying to change my life overnight. I wanted sustainable change and not to be chasing a quick fix which wasn't possible. Once I took the pressure off myself to radically change my life overnight, I began to make smaller changes. Once I started to make smaller changes, I saw results. One of the first changes I wanted to make was reducing my stress levels. I began to implement a daily gratitude practice which involved writing down three things I was grateful for each day, I was more consistent with working on my goals (such as writing my first book) and I didn't feel as stressed. Once the gratitude practice had been implemented and felt habitual, I began to look into yoga classes. I found a studio and enrolled in a beginner's yoga class. The classes allowed me to focus on my breath, being in the moment and moving my body gently. By making small changes, I was able to create a mindfulness practice and I realised smaller changes were more effective and lasting than trying to do everything at once.

Just like any journey, there have been challenges. These challenges have helped me build resilience and they've provided inspiration for this book. One of the biggest lessons I learned during my journey is that it's hard enough to change yourself, let alone someone else. When I was learning new concepts I was thinking of how I could convince others to change or suggest tools they could use to solve their problems. The reality is, if we want something to change we cannot force others to change. It is up to us, as the individual, to change. Whether that is through our behaviours, beliefs, or how we respond to the situation, it is on us. We can have conversations with others and provide them feedback, but we cannot force them to change. I encourage you to focus on what you can control which is yourself. Allow others to do their own thing. While I believe that personal development is incredible and I am glad to be on this path, I am not going to try and convince others to join me.

Not everyone will be receptive to personal development concepts. Some people are happy as they are and are not open to learning more. The twenty-three year old version of me wanted everyone to fall in love with personal development and reconnect with themselves. I saw so many advantages to embarking on my personal development journey and I wanted to persuade others to go on the journey with me. It took a year or so for me to accept that I could not force anyone to join me. Instead, I chose to focus my efforts on writing my first book to those who were beginning their personal development journey and starting to make changes in their life. If people wanted to ask questions about what I was doing or the changes I had made I'd discuss it with them, but I had let go of trying to force personal development concepts onto others. While it's nice to take others with you on the journey, it's important to remember that they're also on their own path and may not be ready or willing to embark on the journey with you.

Once you've moved through the Learning Stage and have begun to make solid changes through the Experimentation and Evaluation Stages, you will likely reach the point where things are flowing. You feel comfortable moving between the stages as needed while continuing your journey. Now you have experience, a toolkit or framework to follow, and you feel comfortable in the journey. If something challenging comes up you know how to use your toolkit to find a way to navigate the challenge or move between these stages to find a new solution.

Affirmations:

1. I am on my own journey.
2. I embrace the highs and lows of my journey.
3. I am focused on bettering myself.
4. I am not in competition with anyone else except me.
5. I am a lifelong learner.

Journal Prompts:

1. What do I do once I've collected information about a subject? Do I keep learning, or do I begin to act?
2. Which stage am I in (Awareness, Learning, Experimentation)?
3. Do I perceive personal development as being a destination to reach or a lifelong journey? Why?
4. Am I willing to test out new things to see what does and doesn't work?
5. Do I try to convince others to follow my path? Why or why not?

Activity:

Write down five things you have learned on your journey so far. How did you learn these things? Was it from a life experience, a book, a podcast, or something else? How have you grown from what you've learned?

Lesson Thirteen: Do The Thing Anyway Because People Don't Care As Much As You Think They Do.

You probably wouldn't worry about what people think of you if you could know how seldom they do. - Olin Miller.

How many times throughout your life have you not done something for fear of judgement from others? I have lost count. It saddens me knowing how many times I have not done something for fear of how the action or I would be perceived. The thing is, I don't think others particularly care.

People don't care as much as we think they do. We've created a story in our head that others are more invested in our lives than they really are. That doesn't mean people don't care about what you do or that you're unloved, but we are all living our own lives. We generally don't have the time to get caught up in the going's on of others to the extent we might think.

You may have noticed this when you've shared something that holds a lot of meaning to you with someone else. They may have been engaged during the conversation, but afterwards, they never mention it again. With so much going on each day, your news may not be of the same level of importance to them, but it doesn't mean they don't care about you.

Like majority of us, I try to listen and show my enthusiasm when someone shares good news with me. That enthusiasm may not extend to me checking in later to see how they are going. It's not because I don't care about them, it's because I don't always have the time to think deeply about what's happening in someone else's life. We all lead busy lives and with some many different things striving for our attention, it can be easy to overlook something.

I can still recall comments made by others from years ago. I've given weight to their words irrespective of whether they were positive or negative. I've held onto them yet, the people who spoke those words have likely forgotten.

When you begin to reflect on how much time you spend thinking about others, you may realise that others aren't spending as much time thinking about you as you think they are. When I realised this, I felt relieved. I would spend a lot of time considering how others would perceive a decision I was going to make – only to find out afterwards that it didn't bother them.

Feeling like others don't care about your achievements as much as you do may hurt, understandably but I'd encourage you to reflect on how much you think about others and their achievements. Each of us has our own life. We have our own fears, problems, hopes, and dreams to focus on. Many of us are self-focused and given the choice we'd opt to focus our time and energy into our own lives rather than judging and commenting on others. If you are spending a great deal of time focusing on what others are or aren't doing in their lives, it's time you could otherwise be spending focusing on yours.

There have likely been times in your life when someone has cared significantly about the decisions you made. That may be why you have created the story that everyone cares about every action you make as much as that person did in that situation. If you're someone who doesn't enjoy letting others down or disappointing someone, you likely take this into consideration when making decisions. It may feel selfish if you're not used to putting yourself first but I encourage you to do so. As we're told by flight attendants, "Fix your own oxygen mask before helping others." This is important when you're making decisions which will have an impact on your life. Consider the impact your decisions may have on others but keep yourself at the front of mind.

You may be confident and steadfast in your decisions. If you are – amazing! If not, it is a skill which can be learned. I tend to find that people who are more empathetic and self-aware struggle with doing things which make them happy. It may be due to the deeply embedded desire to please others, to be perceived in a certain manner, to be accepted, to be worthy of love (albeit conditional love), or because we are uncertain of what we want so it's easier to say no and blame someone else. At twenty-nine, I decided to do something different with my hair. I decided it was time to grow out my fringe. I'd often joked about being born with a fringe and it was part of my identity for twenty-nine years. I had different types of fringes ranging from a wispy fringe to a side fringe. It was a metaphorical safety blanket because I was able to hide behind my fringe.

Seeing as I'd always had a fringe, I expected to receive a lot of comments when I started growing it out. My forehead was no longer covered by a fringe. It was exposed – for all to see. Do you know how many comments I received? Just two. I'll admit my ego was like, "Okay, cool. No one has noticed this not having a fringe thing. Does it look bad?" Then I realised that people don't care as much as I thought they would. What feels like a life changing thing for you may have little impact on others. If I had said I was quitting my job, that would've likely illicit responses from others because my decision would impact them.

How many things had I chosen not to do for fear of how others would react? It would be more things than I'd care to admit. I almost didn't write my first book for that very reason. I was terrified to put something out into the world which felt so raw and vulnerable. It felt like I would be exposed and open to judgement, both good and bad, from people I knew well to strangers who were willing to purchase my book. My desire to be an author and share what I had learned was thankfully stronger than the fear of judgement from others. Since its publication I've had strangers message me to thank for me for writing the book and that it helped them. I've also had positive words from people who know me. I'm going to guess that if you've put something out into the world that felt terrifying to do that it was well-received or you were at least supported by those close to you.

While I've become more self-assured over the years, I have tried to take the thoughts of others (perceived or known) into consideration when I've made decisions. As human being's it's natural to crave connection. We want to fit in, even if that means changing our appearance or how we behave. We hide parts of our true selves to feel like we belong. We may choose to suppress our dreams for fear of how others perceive it. There may even be something hiding underneath that fear. For me, it's a fear of rejection. Other things that could be hiding underneath that fear include abandonment, loss of a relationship, loss of reputation or credibility.

Are you willing to compromise your dreams and desires because someone might make a judgemental comment? Are you willing to compromise your life for fear of how you may or may not be perceived by others? What matters more to you, fulfilling a dream or the words that someone may or may not say to you about it? Hiding parts of your identity can be exhausting because you're keeping up a façade. In contrast, people who are themselves have a beautiful energy surrounding them and they show others that they can be their true selves too.

Affirmations:

1. I am making decisions that serve me.
2. I trust my own voice.
3. I am allowed to put myself first.
4. I am supported.
5. I trust myself.

Journal Prompts:

1. What choices have you made or not made based on the opinion of others?
2. Were these choices in their best interest or yours?
3. How much do you think people care about your life and the decisions you make?
4. Are you comfortable putting yourself first when making decisions? Why or why not?

Activities:

1. Reflect on a time when you did something because of what others said/their opinions. How did you feel about your decision? What was the consequence of listening to their opinions? Did anyone make any comments after you made the decision?
2. Reflect on a time when you didn't do something because of what others said/their opinions. How did you feel about your decision? What was the consequence of not listening to their opinions? Did anyone make any comments after you made the decision?
3. Compare your answers to the above two questions. Are there any differences or similarities between them? Did people react the way you expected them to?

Lesson Fourteen: When The Opinions Of Others Are Drowning Out Your Own.

Don't let the noise of others' drown out your own inner voice. - Steve Jobs.

I've found that people will try and talk you out of something that they feel isn't sensible. For the most part, I believe people do this out of love and concern because they want what is best for us. We can't always rely on others to know what is right for us because they aren't us. They may have an idea of who they think we are and what we need but it's only their perception. It is not our truth. Each of us is multifaceted and as we go through life we discover the people, places, and things that light us up.

People may try to talk you out of something because of their own thoughts, feelings, and limiting beliefs. This could be mirroring your own fears and doubts back to you or someone projecting their own fears and thoughts onto you. Mirroring is when a person is listening to you and will imitate body posture and attitudes. Projecting is when a person places their own traits or emotions onto you. Both are often done subconsciously. When you disrupt the status quo, others may be surprised. They may have thought you were happy with the way things were, unaware of how you truly felt or what you were working towards.

I've travelled by myself, lived overseas, changed jobs, started and closed a business, written a book (excluding this one) amongst other things. Each of us has accomplished many things in our lives and not all of these accomplishments would have been expected by others. You're allowed to do what's right for yourself. Live life on your own terms and go after the dreams that are on your heart.

When I decided to live in Canada for six months when I was twenty-two some thought I was brave for going by myself and others thought I should stay put. While I was living in Canada, I shared photos and people could see how happy I was. Their opinions changed and they were supportive. When I returned home, my mum told me she didn't want me to go but wasn't going to stop me because she knew it was something I needed to do. I knew that if I didn't go then, I wouldn't go. I wasn't willing to let others talk me out of something I felt so strongly about. I knew I needed to do it for me. The choices you make in life may not make sense to others but if it feels right for you, go for it. There is a reason why you're being pulled so strongly to do something, and you owe it to yourself to explore it.

I'm the kind of person who will ask for input when I'm unsure of what I should do, but other than that I am headstrong in going after what I want. If you tend to be persuaded by the opinions of others and want to learn how to be less persuaded, read on. The more you make decisions independently, the easier it becomes. You learn to listen to and trust your own voice. Remember, it's your life and you know yourself better than anyone else.

External validation is when a person seeks recognition, affirmation, or confirmation of their strengths and achievements from others. Those who seek validation solely from others will likely feel discontent. It's a gamble to wait for validation from others before you allow yourself to feel good about yourself, your decisions, or your achievements. If you are chasing validation from others and don't receive it, you may feel empty or disappointed. You may be doing things to your own detriment to appease others and gain their recognition. It can also be tiring for your loved ones who may feel like they need to constantly affirm your strengths and achievements.

Internal validation is when you are aware of your own strengths, acknowledge your own achievements, and back yourself. You seek validation from yourself without having to rely on others to affirm or celebrate you before you believe you are worthy of being affirmed or celebrated.

If we think of validation as a cake, you can either make the cake yourself (internal validation) or wait for someone to make one for you (external validation). With internal validation there is an opportunity for external validation to add to the experience. Maybe you'll be complimented on the cake you made. Maybe you will get two cakes! The external validation is an extra cherry on top. With or without it, you still got the cake you wanted.

If you are a more confident person and know your worth, you'll likely seek validation from within yourself rather than from others. If you rely on external validation, you may have days when you feel worthy and other days... not so much. It's a volatile cycle to be in. This is because you are relying on others to affirm you, your strengths, and your accomplishments before you can acknowledge them yourself.

You can begin to increase your focus on internal validations, and reduce your reliance on external validation by:

- Looking inwards, learning what is important to you, and standing by it.
- Write down a list of your strengths to remind yourself what you are good at.
- Say the things you'd want others to say to you to yourself.
- Celebrate your achievements.
- Empower yourself to make your own decisions. Start small and

keep building on this.

Have you every shared something you're excited about with someone only to feel disappointed and deflated after? I equate it to holding a balloon only to have someone walk up and pop it. This is another example of seeking external validation.

For the most part, when you share your goals with others and they respond in a way that leaves you feeling deflated, it isn't because they're trying to hurt you. They're often trying to protect you and have your best interests at heart. However, if someone is consistently diminishing your goals it may be worth having a conversation with them to address how it makes you feel. If their behaviour remains unchanged, you can stop sharing your goals and ideas with them.

It's worthwhile looking at what you expect from others in terms of their response. Say you've just announced your engagement and a loved one says, "That's nice." If your loved one hasn't said the words you expected them to say, you might internalise it as they're not happy for you. You might allow their response to influence how you feel about your engagement. A good question to ask yourself is, "Did I do this for them or for myself?"

If you were content with internal validation, the congratulatory reactions from others would be a bonus. When Jesse and I purchased our house we were both incredibly proud of what we'd achieved. When we shared the news with others their opinions of what the house looked like didn't bother us because we were happy with the choice we made.

Does that mean you don't care what others think? I do. I value and take the opinions of others into consideration where it's appropriate, but the weight I give to their opinion has decreased. Similarly, my expectation of receiving a certain response from others has also decreased. I'm no longer yearning for the external validation I used to. If I feel certain of a decision I've made, I'm prepared to back myself. If I have the support of others, that's a bonus. If I don't receive the support of others, it won't necessarily stop me from doing what I feel is right.

There are times in our lives when we feel strongly about a decision. It may not make sense to others, but you know that it's the right one for you. When you can stand steadfast in your decision, go for it! Regardless of what others say or think. Not everyone will have the same vision as you and their opinions may be based in fear or it may be a projection of something they wish they had done. Whatever the reason, you can either allow yourself to be talked out of what you truly want to do, or you can do the thing anyway.

Whether it's starting a new job, business, moving houses, moving to a different country, or setting a different goal, you get to choose whether you go for it or not. No one can stop you from taking action, except yourself. It may be difficult at first but once you start to make progress, it's worth it. You'll be glad you didn't let others talk you out of something you truly wanted to do. Sometimes doing the thing proves to others that you were serious about it, and they'll see the impact it has on your life. Not everyone sees your vision at the same time you do. Perhaps you've experienced a moment like this in your life. A moment where you felt self-assured and knew you were going to do the thing. Even if was scary, even if it meant stepping into the unknown, or possibly disappointing someone.

One of the biggest things which helped me was being quiet with the decisions you're making. Rather than telling people what you're going to do beforehand. Wait until you've made the decision and let them know after the fact. I'm not saying that you can't talk to anyone about the decisions you're making. However, it could be beneficial to limit who and how many people you involve in the process. Not all decisions you make require input from others. I have found that this strategy works because you're empowering yourself to make the decision and then the opinion of others becomes feedback instead of never knowing what your own opinion is outside of the influence of others.

If you feel strongly about a decision you're making or have made, you don't need to justify it to others. People may not understand why you've done it, but they don't always need to. You know your life inside and out. You're the one living the situation. Others only have an inkling of what you're experiencing.

A perfect example of this is if you want to change jobs. From the outside looking in, others may perceive you to have the ideal job, work-life balance, and great colleagues. Yet if you're discontent in the job then it makes sense that you'd want to find something else. It's not your responsibility to stay in an unfulfilling job to appease others. When you're ready to move on to a new job or change your career, there will be people who want you to stay. Common reasons include not disrupting the status quo, it's comfortable and familiar having you there, someone leaving may mean more work for others to do, or it might change the dynamics of the workplace. You deserve to live a fulfilling life and be in environments which make you feel good, even if that goes against the perceptions others hold of you.

The choice is simple but not always easy. You can choose who you share your news or goals with, and when. Some may feel like they're being left out of the loop but it's your choice who you share your news with. If you're wanting to share it with others who can share your excitement, go for it. If you want to keep the news from people who you feel would lovingly try to talk you out of it, go for it.

I understand this isn't always simple when it comes to family. If you want to keep sharing your life with your family but you feel they aren't supporting you in the way you want, have the conversation. I know it isn't easy to let them know how you're feeling, but chances are they don't even know you're upset about it. Communicate clearly and if they still respond the same way, you can choose whether you restrict what you tell them.

When I was deciding whether to enrol in a Commerce degree or an Arts degree at University I sought advice from my parents. I adore my parents and between wanting to make them proud and wanting to find a safe job after getting my degree, I ended up enrolling in the Commerce degree. To this day I have not been in a role which has required me to use my degree. At times I wonder what would have happened if I had followed my passion of media and enrolled in the Arts degree instead. While I don't blame my parents for the decision I made. I do want to shed light on how others, especially our loved ones, can influence our decisions when we aren't aware of it.

If I hadn't enrolled in the Commerce degree, I may not have found out about the internation exchange program which led me to Canada and then led me back home to where I met Jesse. Life unfolds as it's meant to and sometimes what feels like the wrong choice looking back was really a catalyst to get you to where you were meant to be.

Now that I have a better understanding of how others can influence my decisions, I have found ways to trust myself. I have learned more about myself, my motives for making decisions and my natural decision-making process. I'm no longer willing to make big decisions that make others feel comfortable if it's at the expense of myself. It isn't selfish to make decisions that are good for you. Others may need to adjust and accept it but that is their responsibility, not yours. Life is short, listen to your own voice.

Not sure what to wear? Post a poll on social media to have others decide for you. Not sure whether you should break up with your partner? Ask your friends for guidance. Whether it's a life changing decision or a smaller one, we often turn to others. We want others to tell us what we should do. This could be a result of analysis paralysis when you've analysed a decision (quick pro con list, anyone?) and you cannot decide which decision will yield the best outcome. Other times, it's because we don't trust ourselves with the decision or if we deflect the decision to others, we can hold them accountable for the outcome rather than ourselves.

How do we begin to break the cycle of asking others for permission or guidance? Start small. Begin to empower yourself to make decisions. Allow yourself to be self-led. This process takes time and while there is a time and place for soliciting the opinions of others, not every decision requires external input or validation. By empowering yourself to make decisions, you get to build your self-belief. You begin to trust that you can make your own decisions whilst having your best interests in mind. At the end of the day, you know yourself better than anyone (even on the days when it may not feel like it). You know how you feel about a situation – even when it may not be completely obvious at first.

We often look to others for validation when the answer is within us. At the end of the day, we know how we feel about a situation, whether we want to admit it or not. Sometimes, that feeling is intense and other times, it's like a whisper. It's there, you just need to be willing to trust yourself.

Affirmations:

1. I make decisions which feel good for me.
2. I am allowed to make decisions that support me to grow and expand.
3. I am not responsible for how others perceive the choices I make.
4. I know myself best and I make informed decisions.
5. I trust myself to make decisions.

Journal prompts:

1. Am I comfortable listening to my own voice or am I easily persuaded by the thoughts and feelings of others?

2. Recall a time when you made a decision based on the opinions of others. Did it feel like you made the right decision for you? Why or why not?

3. Do you involve others in your decision-making process? If so, who and how much weight do you give to their opinions?

4. Have you made a decision based on your own thoughts and feelings which surprised others? Did you feel empowered? Did you want to change your decision after their feedback?

5. Why do I ask others for their opinion about a decision I am making? Is it because I want them to affirm that I am making the right decision or to get an outsider's perspective?

Activities:

1. The next time you're making a big decision, write a list of who you will share the news with before you've made the decision. Notice how you allow their opinions to influence your decision. Once the decision has been made, do you feel comfortable accepting that if you're happy with the decision that's all that you need? If not, who are you wanting to seek external validation from and how do you feel if you do or don't get it?

2. Begin a gratitude journal and write down three things you're grateful for each day. Where possible, try and write down three different things each day. This will help you to reflect on your day and notice the smaller things (such as someone holding a door open for you) that you can be grateful for. Over time, you may find yourself actively searching for moments to be grateful for. As a result of being open to experiences to be grateful for, you may notice that these moments happen more often.

3. When you next feel yourself reaching for your phone to ask for someone else's opinion on a situation or decision in your life, take

a moment to decide what you think first. If you still want to ask for their input or guidance, reach out to them. You can share your thoughts on the situation and what you're thinking of doing and then ask for their input.

Part Three: Evolving And Growing As Our Own Entity.

Lesson Fifteen: You Are Responsible For Your Actions and Choices.

Take responsibility. It's where your powers live. - Will Craig.

If you want to change your life, you'll need to learn how to be accountable for your choices and actions. It's as simple and complicated as that.

Accountability takes courage because it isn't easy to stand up and own a mistake, especially if others are involved. It may feel easier to blame others or the situation than take responsibility for your part, but when you do you give away your personal power. When I talk about giving away your personal power, I'm referring to a person who believes they don't have any choice or influence over their life or the decisions they make. This belief is often subconscious.

You've likely met a person who takes zero accountability for their mistakes, actions, and decisions. They deflect blame, claim they are perfect and could never make a mistake. If you have encountered a person who appears to lack accountability, it is not your responsibility to fix them. You can provide ideas and suggestions for how they could perceive a situation differently, but it is ultimately their decision whether they want to make a change or not. Not everyone is willing to embrace their imperfections or admit when they've made a mistake. Not everyone is willing to be responsible for their actions and take accountability. It is not your responsibility to try and change these individuals. It's their life and if they want to live in this way, that is their choice.

Perhaps there have even been times in your life when you have been this person. There have certainly been times in my life when I have not been accountable for my actions. I would blame the situation or another person because I wasn't willing to acknowledge my own actions. In that moment, it was easier for me to deflect blame onto others. I can't recall a specific moment when I was prepared to start looking at my own actions but once I did, I realised it was a better way to live. I quickly learned that nothing would change until I started to take accountability for my decisions – including the good and the bad.

During my early twenties, I was single. I didn't mind being single for the most part. Until it came to family events and weddings when I suddenly felt like a third wheel. I felt lonely and it was easier to be a victim of my circumstances and think, "I'm unlovable. Who would ever want to be with me", then it was to put myself out there and go on a date. Unsurprisingly, I didn't attract anyone into my life with this perspective. People would ask why I was single and I'd say I was happy being on my own. The truth, one which I didn't want to admit to myself at the time, was that I feared being vulnerable. Dating seemed awkward and uncomfortable. Rather than share that fear with others I put on an independent and loving it persona.

It wasn't until I started to feel comfortable in my own skin and started living life from that place that I attracted a partner. Arguably, I didn't actively go out in search of a boyfriend. But I did decide to start socialising more which led to meeting Jesse at a mutual friend's birthday party. If I hadn't changed my perspective, I likely would've skipped the party and stayed at home.

When you don't take responsibility for your actions you tend to think that life is happening to you rather than for you. You take the traffic jams, hard times, and failures personally. You can quickly adopt a victim mentality. A person who has a victim mentality believes they are powerless to control the outcome of their life. They are a victim of their circumstances.

I don't know about you, but I don't want to feel powerless over my life's trajectory. To alter your mindset and take your personal power back, you begin by taking accountability for your actions. Life happens in duality. There will be good times and bad times. It's inevitable. We can choose to be a victim of our circumstances, or we can take responsibility for them. Arguably, one will leave you disempowered and the other will empower you. The choice is yours.

My mum was in a job that she tolerated for over a decade. My dad, sister, and I could see that she wasn't happy and knew she deserved to be in a job which she enjoyed but we couldn't change her mind. We couldn't make her see her worth until she was ready to see it for herself. Until she was ready, we held space for her to talk about work and how it wasn't enjoyable. One day, she was ready to start looking for another job. She was ready to take accountability for her situation and open to changing it. She realised she deserved better and was willing to make it happen.

We supported her through the process and she was offered a new job. I remember speaking to her on the phone after she was offered the role. She was elated with the offer, but it was only for a three-month contract with a possibility of an extension. She said she was going to turn down the job because she wasn't comfortable leaving a permanent role for the unknown. What if in three months she no longer had a job? I understood where she was coming from and so we talked it out. I asked her if she wanted to be in the same job in five years' time. She said no. I asked a few more questions to help her unpack her feelings and she decided to say yes to the new role. After the initial three months her contract was extended and she was subsequently offered a permanent position. It all worked out.

I couldn't change my mum's mind and she had a perfectly good list of reasons why she should have turned down the role. The reasons were logical yet, knowing my mum well, I could tell that these reasons came from a place of uncertainty, fear, and doubt. Having seen how excited she was when she had the interview and was offered the role, I knew there was a part of her which was willing to seize the opportunity, regardless of the perceived risk. There will be times in life when you'll need to consider which risk you'd prefer to take. The risk of staying in the same place, knowing how you feel about it, or the risk of saying yes to something new.

If you are in a position where you can offer space to a loved one to talk through their decision-making process, it's important to listen and not persuade. Ask questions without judgement and allow the person to come to their own conclusion. It may be difficult when you want them to make a certain decision because you can see it will benefit them. However, it's best to let them make their own decision. They are the ones that need to be ready to step forward into this new experience. While we can offer support, it is not our job to decide for the other person. That disempowers them. We want them to feel accountable for their own decisions so they can own it.

I share these stories to show how a victim mentality can limit us and how taking accountability can provide us with great opportunities and a sense of empowerment. I understand life isn't always easy but during the challenges you can choose how you respond to the situation. You can choose to be a victim and focus on what has happened. Or you can choose to empower yourself by focusing on moving forward and through it.

If you choose the latter, you'll be adopting a growth mindset. Dr Carol Dweck explains that "in a growth mindset, people believe that their most basic abilities can be developed through dedication and hard work – brains and talent are just the starting point." Such a mindset enables individuals to get through challenges and setbacks. Rather than complaining about a situation and playing the victim, a person with a growth mindset will look for the lesson and take accountability. They'll make changes and know that they're not helpless.

Changing your mindset won't happen overnight so please be kind to yourself as you learn to navigate situations differently. It takes time to unlearn engrained behaviours. You may not always be able to catch yourself when you begin to fall into the role of the victim. When you do notice yourself deflecting blame to others or reacting to a situation rather than responding, take a breath and see if you can excuse yourself. If you can step back from the situation, reflect on how a person who takes accountability for their actions would respond and speak accordingly. If you are unable to excuse yourself from the situation, try to change your response and consider where you can be accountable. Being accountable doesn't mean you have to accept responsibility for the thoughts, feelings, and choices made by others. It means you take responsibility for your own actions.

You may notice others who have a victim mindset and want to help them change. When this urge arises, please be kind with that person. Not everyone is ready, willing, or able to change their mindset or have a deeper level of self-awareness. Focus your energy on changing what is within your control (how you respond) and you may be surprised by how others change their responses to mirror yours.

When you can take responsibility for your own actions, you will find solutions faster. You no longer focus on blaming others for what has happened and instead, you focus your efforts on moving forward. When there are challenges in life, you'll be better equipped to handle them and likely, overcome the challenges faster than if you had a victim mindset.

Affirmations:

1. I am powerful beyond measure.
2. I am responsible for my own thoughts, feelings, and actions.
3. I am willing to accept my part in situations.
4. I choose to fail forward and learn from my mistakes.
5. I am accountable and act with integrity.

Journal Prompts:

1. Describe a time you were accountable for your actions. How did you feel?
2. Describe a time when you deflected responsibility to others. How did you feel in that situation?
3. Do you currently take responsibility for your actions? Why or why not?

Activities:

1. If you aren't sure how you deal with challenging situations and are open to finding out how others perceive your response, ask 1-3 people to give you feedback. By seeking feedback from people you trust, you can start to see how you have responded previously and whether there are any patterns of behaviour that you might want to change in the future.
2. If you have identified times when you have had a victim mentality, journal on how a person with a victim mindset and growth mindset would deal with the situation. This will allow you to open your perspective so if a challenging situation arises you can think of new ways to handle it.
3. Write down your definition of personal power. How would that

person act, feel, and look like? If you feel that you are not this person and would like to be, what steps can you take to become them?

Lesson Sixteen: You're More Than A Number On A Scale.

Know that you are so much more than the value you place on your body. It's not the only thing that defines you. - Molly Tarlov.

You are worthy of loving yourself. Your value as a person does not depend on how much you weigh and when you choose to love your body over guilting yourself and shaming your body, you will likely feel more confident and content. As someone who used to focus on losing weight and not feeling worthy even at my lowest weight, I get how impossible the previous sentence may seem to you.

It breaks my heart to think back to the time I allowed a number on the scale to dictate how I felt about my body and self-worth. The missed beach swims, lack of body confidence, and not feeling comfortable in my own skin. Irrespective of gender, there are expectations about how each of us should look. If you fail to meet the expectations, then you're deemed not worthy. At least, that's how the narrative in many magazines and advertisements is constructed. We, as individuals have the power to rewrite that narrative and embrace all the things that make us unique.

Women are bombarded with advertisements and media content which encourages us to change how we look. From make-up products to plastic surgery and weight loss products, it can be challenging to believe you are worthy exactly as you are. I truly believe we are all loveable and enough as we are in any given moment, but my belief is not yours. It is up to you to decide what you want to believe about yourself. If you want to change how you feel about yourself, you have the power to do so.

It is implied that women are to be small and quiet. While I feel like this ideology is slowly changing, if you grew up in a generation which encouraged this way of being and thinking, it can be challenging to change this belief. Be confident in who you are and you'll encourage others to do the same. Let's create a movement where we embrace who we are and feel inherently worthy of love, kindness, and being… irrespective of how our bodies look.

This lesson was one I didn't truly learn until my mid to late twenties. I want to provide a trigger warning to anyone who has or is experiencing an eating disorder as the following paragraphs involve parts of my own story and relationship with food.

Throughout my school life, I was bullied because of my weight. When I was thirteen, I got braces and I used that as an excuse to stop eating some of the foods I did previously. I lost weight and discovered counting calories. This habit soon became automatic and it was one that I held onto for fifteen or so years.

I became obsessed. I weighed myself every single day. I was never small enough. If I gained weight, I decided to obsess over it. What was it that I ate the previous day that made me gain weight? To compensate for the weight gain, I'd exercise longer and eat less. I didn't consider that our body weights fluctuate each day and given that we are made up of 70% water, of course our weight isn't going to stay the same each day. At the time, I didn't even consider that. I was purely focused on the numbers.

Even at my lowest weight of 47 kilograms at age twenty-four, I still wanted to weigh less. While I was never formally diagnosed with an eating disorder, food ruled my life. I had so many rules around what I would and wouldn't eat. I over-exercised to make up for the days when I 'let myself go' by binge eating. It was a way of life which quietly consumed me. There wasn't space for other thoughts because I was heavily focused on my eating patterns. I wanted to control every portion and if I felt that control slipping away, I would become upset. It showed up in my relationships with Jesse, my family and friends. I would research menus and if there wasn't a salad option available, I would freak out. Burgers, pizza, pasta, rice – they were all bad. I found substitutes for pasta and rice to lower the calorie amount of the food. I'd only cook recipes which had nutritional information available. To that younger version of me, that was what healthy looked like.

At twenty-five, I gained 10 kilograms in the space of a month. I freaked out. I felt like I had lost control. My self-confidence took a massive hit and I was scared that others wouldn't love me because I had gained weight. Based on past experiences in school, I had created a story in my mind which I believed without question for nearly fifteen years. If I'm skinny, I'll be likeable and if I'm larger, I won't be.

I didn't return to my status quo weight until I was twenty-seven. During those next two years, I tried different fad diets, saw a naturopath, and read books to try and figure out why I had gained the weight and how I could lose it. I wasn't seeing any results from the change in my diet, and I was told to go into a calorie deficit to lose the weight by a GP and naturopath. As soon as that option was suggested to me, there was something deep inside me which said, "No." It was an internal "No", but it was so strong. I knew that wasn't the answer and I didn't want to fall back into my old habit of depriving myself of food. I just wanted to feel like myself again.

The experience gave me an opportunity to reflect on how I was treating myself. I didn't realise how much of my self-worth was based on a number on a scale. It was conditional self-love, and I knew that

I deserved more from myself. I started to find ways to accept myself as I was. It wasn't easy trying to create a new story and breaking old patterns of behaviour. If I hadn't gained the weight like I did, I wouldn't have had the opportunity to change my relationship with food or myself. I needed that situation to shake me awake and help me find a new way of thinking and being.

I managed to pinpoint the issue and once addressed, I returned to my status quo weight. I had blood tests done and discovered that my iron levels were around 17μg/L. After a few months on iron tablets as well as continuing with my usual exercise routine and eating, the weight fell away. I wasn't weighing myself, but I noticed that my clothes began to fit better again and clothes I had outgrown, I was able to wear again. To release control of counting calories and being obsessed with my weight was not an easy journey. There were many days when I felt helpless, sad, and unworthy. There were days when I was tempted to fall back into my old habits. On those days, I affirmed myself and started to accept how I looked.

Everyone is different so I can only speak from personal experience here. It's been roughly four years since I began to change my relationship with food and in turn, myself. I didn't consciously realise I had a problem until I had an appointment with a dietician. That was the moment I knew something had to change. Rewiring your brain to change your stories and deeply held beliefs is not easy. Yes, there will be days when the old story doesn't pop up and that feels amazing, but there will likely be situations which will challenge you. For instance, if you're someone who used to avoid certain foods out of fear it would lead to weight gain, you may have days when you suppress a craving due to this thought. I still have moments (thankfully, they're a rare occasion now) when the old story comes back. With time, it gets easier and you become more aware. If you are just starting to change your story or are in the middle of it, keep going. You have got this.

I believe we all have a status quo weight, a weight which we don't need to try hard to maintain. As each of us is different, our status quo weights will vary. I like to define the status quo weight as 'the amount you weigh when you're maintaining your regular diet and exercise regime'. It's the weight you are when you don't have to be in a calorie deficit or working out more than usual to lose weight or gain muscle mass.

Each of us deserves to feel comfortable in our skin. We all have flaws and that's what makes each of us unique and beautiful. Many of us are acutely aware of our flaws – the blemishes, stretch marks, the wrinkles, the unwanted hair but you know what? Most other people don't even notice! It's because they're focused on their flaws too. Your value and self-worth cannot be measured by a weight on the scale. If you are focused on counting calories and wanting to lose weight, I'd lovingly encourage you to ask yourself why.

- Why do I want to lose weight?
- Do I believe I'll be judged or loved less if I weigh more?
- Do I believe I won't be safe if I weigh less?
- Am I willing to accept my body as she is right now?
- Am I willing to believe I can be loved unconditionally?

If you are reading this lesson and it's bringing up strong emotions for you, I'd encourage you to reach out to a loved one or a professional for support. It is possible to choose a new way of thinking and to have a healthier relationship with food (one where you don't obsess over every meal). It may not be the easiest of journeys but the mental freedom I've experienced after is worth it.

Affirmations:

1. I am allowed to take up space.
2. I am worthy of being seen and heard.
3. I am allowed to share my story.
4. I am beautiful inside and out.
5. I nourish and nurture my body.

Journal Prompts:

1. List five of your characteristics you admire.
2. How do you measure your self-worth? Is it a metric you'd like to change?
3. When was the last time that you felt comfortable in your own skin? What emotions did you feel? How did you dress? How did you show up in your relationships and for yourself?
4. If it's been a while since you've felt comfortable in your own skin, what is something you can do this week to feel better about yourself?
5. What does self-love mean to you?
6. If you're an all-in kind of person (rather than someone who can moderate), are there any habits which may have a negative impact or don't align with your values that you want to change, remove or replace?
7. If you count calories or plan every meal, does this occupy a lot of space in your brain? Can you remember a time when you weren't thinking about food to the extent you currently are? Is there a difference?

Activity:

If you're up for a challenge, I want you to write down an affirmation which helps you feel confident and worthy. For the next 30 days, I want you to stick it somewhere you'll see it several times a day and say it out loud each time you see it.

If negative thoughts pop up, be gentle with yourself. It's normal for the old story to try and make a comeback. It's what you've known for a while so when you're trying to reprogram it (with the help of affirmations), your old story feels threatened.

Lesson Seventeen: When You Get The Chance, Travel Or Live Elsewhere.

Travel changes you. As you move through this life and this world you change things slightly, you leave marks behind, however small., And in return, life-and travel-leaves marks on you. - Anthony Bourdain.

Travel is one of the few things in life which gives you a high return on your investment. After each trip you return home with a deeper appreciation for the world, your place in it, and how others live. Let's not forget how soothing it is to be back in your own bed and have a home cooked meal.

Travel forces us to be physically removed from our usual routine and to quickly adapt to our new surroundings. We learn to immerse ourselves in another location and culture. Time becomes borrowed and you appreciate the moments in that place because you know you only have a limited time there. In contrast, how many times have you put off visiting somewhere near your hometown because you can do it at any time. Any time just hasn't arrived yet. That's the beauty of travel. You either do the thing while you're there or you don't. Time is precious, the moments are lived in, and you adapt to your surroundings in no time at all.

Do you feel like you have a greater awareness of time or the perceived lack of time while you're on holiday? As soon as we land at our destination we are on a countdown to when we return home. Perhaps you're like me in the sense that that thought encourages you to really immerse yourself in the moment and enjoy it. Perhaps you even find that there isn't necessarily a bad day when you're travelling because you are grateful for being there.

I'm not here to try and convince you to travel. If travel is not a value of yours feel free to move onto the next chapter in this book. I appreciate that some are comfortable with life as it is and they're not wanting to travel for their own reasons. There's no judgement from me. As someone who does enjoy traveling, I respect that not everyone will share the same opinion as me on the topic.

If travel is a value of yours, I also understand that not everyone has the means or desire to travel overseas. You can still explore your own state or country. Not only does travel give you an opportunity to break free from your standard routine, but it also encourages you to seek out adventure, to experience new things, and meet new people.

When I was single in my early twenties, I travelled domestically around Australia and went on road trips in my home state of Western Australia. Some people were surprised that I was going on my own and thought I was brave for doing so. All I thought was that I wasn't going to let not having a partner keep me from exploring new places and living life according to one of my highest values.

My commitment to my values was a strong pulling force for me saying yes to the working holiday in Canada. While that life changing trip was nearly eight years ago, it was such a pivotal experience.

During my time in Canada, I learned a lot about myself. As someone who is normally quite shy, I felt I was able to come out of my shell and make new friends all from different countries. We became fast friends because we were all living together. We were having a shared experience which bonded us together and we all looked out for one another.

Travelling to Canada was my first international trip I did on my own. I had to rely on myself to get where I needed to go and I'm proud to say that I navigated it successfully. When I returned to Australia, I felt like I had grown up and discovered more about myself – the good and the bad.

I learned that as cosy as it is living in a small town, gossip spreads quickly. Whether it was a new couple alert, people fighting, or someone wanting to create drama it spread like wildfire. I learned how easy it was for me to get caught up in the gossip and drama. I also learned that I don't like that version of myself and how to adjust my behaviour and standards for myself. I learned that I was capable of navigating around an unknown place, I was able to make new friends and try new things such as snowboarding. I also appreciated time differently because I knew I wouldn't always be living there.

Whether it's a month, six months, a year, or longer living abroad is a life experience. You go beyond living out of a suitcase to trying to create a home base for yourself. You learn about the place, where to go, what to do, and sometimes even what to avoid. You build self-confidence by figuring things out when everything is new. You learn how capable you are on your own and that you can quickly adapt to new situations. You don't see new things as obstacles, instead, you perceive them as an opportunity to learn and grow. There's a thrill from learning new skills.

When you're in a new environment, you tend to adapt to fit in. When you're away from loved ones, you don't have those relationships to fall back on. You can either try and fit in while being true to yourself or be by yourself. In a new environment, you can be anyone you want to be. You can break free of the expectations people have of you and present yourself to the world as you truly are. To do so, you will need to override the default programming of trying to fit in to gain a sense of belonging. This can be challenging to override especially when you're alone and a world away from those who know and love you. I found I observed the group dynamics, stayed quiet and then began to reveal parts of my personality gradually. I was able to present myself as I wanted to be – someone who had a sense of humour, was willing to try new things and make new friends.

If you are considering living overseas, I encourage you to do the research and say yes to the opportunity if it feels right. I purchased a changeable plane ticket when I moved to Canada because I wanted my return flight date to be flexible. I figured, if I got homesick, didn't enjoy living overseas, or wanted to stay longer, I could. If you try it and want to come home, you can. It's a win-win situation. Another option is to by a one-way ticket and set aside money for your flight home. This will give you a similar safety net. I'm not suggesting that is not possible to travel or live abroad when you are older. However, you may find that it isn't as simple as packing a bag and grabbing a plane ticket. There may be more reasons to stay where you are or the process of moving abroad takes additional planning and resources.

If you have an opportunity to live abroad or travel for an extended period, seize it. Some opportunities only come once and if you don't go while you have the chance, you may not go at all. I knew if I didn't go to Canada when I did, I wouldn't have gone. Some of my excuses would have been, "Oh, I can't live overseas because I have a house, a car, a job, a family." While these are all valid points, if you want to make it happen, you will. There are plenty of people in any or all of these situations who have moved overseas to live out their own traveling or living abroad dreams.

Affirmations:

1. I welcome new experiences.

2. Travel opens my mind to new ways of being and doing.
3. I navigate new places with confidence.
4. I embrace the opportunity for self-discovery when travelling independently or with others.
5. My resilience grows with every trip I go on.

Journal prompts:

1. Am I open to living somewhere else in the world? Why or why not?
2. If I could travel anywhere, where would I go?
3. Would I prefer to do a working holiday or travel for a longer period?
4. Would I prefer to travel by myself, with friends, or a partner?
5. Is there anything holding me back (real or perceived) from travelling or living elsewhere?

Activity:

Sit with the following question and do a free journal session to see what comes to mind: If money, time, my circumstances weren't a consideration, would I want to live overseas? If so, where?

If your free journal session on the above question suggested yes, the next question I'd like you to ask yourself is: what would I need to do to make this a reality?

From these two questions, you can ascertain whether it's something you may be interested in and whether it's something you can begin to take action towards. If it isn't, that's perfectly fine too.

Lesson Eighteen: When You Invest Time, Money And Energy In Yourself.

"You are your greatest asset. No ifs, buts or maybes. You are your greatest asset, period."

When was the last time you did something for yourself? Many of us focus on satisfying the needs of others and we overlook our own needs in the process. We invest our time, money and energy into our relationships with ease yet when it comes to the relationship we have with ourselves, we don't make the same investment. If you don't currently spend time, money or energy on yourself, I'd encourage you to reflect on the reasons why.

Do you feel worthy of spending money, time and energy on yourself? I'd love for you to free journal on this for a few minutes. Allow yourself to write down whatever comes into your mind without judgement and see what flows out. Chances are you'll be surprised by what lands on the paper.

It certainly came as a surprise to me when I learned that self-worth, money, time, and energy are all linked. How you invest your money, time, and energy are often a reflection of your feelings of self-worth or lack there-of.

When I was twenty-eight, I began working with a money coach. I had already read several books on money and while these books gave me an idea of how to change my behaviour with money, I didn't make any changes to my mindset, so the changes didn't stick. This time I invested time, money, and energy into the course work. By doing so, I was able to unpack the limiting beliefs I held around money and I realised that my self-worth was linked to my money patterns.

When I looked at how I was spending and investing my money I noticed that it wasn't in alignment with my priorities. I was spending money on things I thought I should be spending money on rather than the things I wanted to. After this realisation, I changed how I was allocating my money and I felt so much better. I was reminded that I was worthy of spending and investing my money on the things I wanted. I then shifted my focus to how I was spending my time and energy.

In recent years, I've had to unpack and re-write several beliefs which had me putting others before myself. I'd willingly spend money and invest time and energy into helping others to the detriment of myself. Now I still help and spend money on others, but I do it from a different place. I invest my time, money, and energy with love and conscious thought rather than out of feelings of obligation and trying to be a people pleaser.

I jokingly say that I am the event planner for my family and at times, Jesse's family because I enjoy getting people together for casual get-togethers and special occasions. For those who are the event planners of their social circles or families, you'll know how much time, energy and at times, money goes into organising these events.

After a while I began to feel resentful for constantly being the one that was organising events. It began to feel like an unwanted job that I had volunteered to take on. No-one named me as the family event planner. It was a role I took on myself and I wasn't sure how to take a step back from it. I felt like it was expected that I would organise events and when I did take a step back, events didn't get organised. I'd then step in and take on the role feeling slightly resentful that in a group of adults no one else was willing to step up and organise an event. Upon reflection, I took this role on because I wanted the external validation. I knew I was good at organising events and I wanted to be accepted by Jesse's family. I thought that if I continued to organise and host events, I'd be perceived as a valuable member of their family.

While I still organise events, I have put forward ideas to take the burden off myself. I suggested to my family and Jesse's family that we start doing a rotating monthly dinner. It allows each person to host a dinner and we all know when we'll be seeing one another. Everyone agreed to the idea and it's working well. Most people have hosted dinners and been active participants. I realised that while I enjoy organising events, it doesn't have to just fall to me.

I share this example because when we do things out of obligation or wanting to please others, it can be exhausting after a while. At first, I felt excited and happy to be organising events but after several years of doing it, the resentment kicked in. I've actively taken a step back from organising events because I realised it is not my responsibility to organise every event. I also realised that I was organising events from a place of people pleasing. I organised family dinners with Jesse's family because I wanted them to accept me into their family and to show that I cared about them. I'd organise events for my family to take the weight off my mum and dad having to host us. I was doing it for others rather than myself.

I still organise and host events, but I don't do it from the same reasons. I do it because I want to get loved ones together and to catch up. It's no longer about wanting to impress others to feel accepted or to help others. When we do host events now, I feel calmer and grateful to have people over because I do it from a place of want, not self-imposed obligation.

If you are someone who tends to put others before themselves, you're not alone. It feels good to help others. But when you're constantly putting others before yourself, you'll likely begin to feel resentful and worn out. As a child you may have been taught to be kind to others and to help when you can. I'm grateful for being taught that as a child because I do believe it's important to be a kind human. However, I feel that we should also be taught that it's equally (if not more) important to take care of yourself. While being kind and helping others out is important, it is also more than okay to put yourself first. It is not your responsibility to save everyone else. Not only is it burdensome, but it is also disempowering for the person you are trying to save.

There have been situations where I have wanted to step in and take over under the guise of helping. I have stopped myself because the other person can do it themselves. I don't need to be involved. I am someone who likes to keep the peace and be a harmonizer (I am a Libra after all!) so this was not an easy habit to break and reform. I share these titbits because I want to remind you it's possible to break an existing habit and form a new one.

Once you begin to invest your money, time, and energy into the things which make you feel good you begin to feel better. The feelings of frustration, obligation, and resentment begin to fade because you're investing on your own terms. When we stop doing things for external validation, we increase our feelings of self-worth because we know we are worthy irrespective of others.

Affirmations:

1. I am worthy of investing time, money, and energy into myself.
2. I am my greatest asset.
3. I choose to invest in myself.
4. I take care of myself so I can perform at my best.
5. I invest wisely.

Journal prompts:

1. How does the thought of spending money on myself make me feel? Why?
2. Do I freely spend time, money, and energy on others? If so, how do I feel afterwards?
3. Am I willing to believe that I am worthy of spending money, time, and energy on myself?
4. Is there something I want to stop or start doing?
5. Do you feel like you need to save others? If so, where has that come from?
6. Do you feel comfortable spending time, money, and energy on yourself? Why or why not?
7. Do you tend to put the needs of others before your own? If so, how do you feel after doing that?

Activity

Write down a list of ways you can invest in yourself. Create a list of ways you can invest money into you, spend time on yourself, and spend energy on yourself. Once you've written the list, pick one item for the current week. Reflect on how you felt before and after you invested the time, money, or energy into yourself. Repeat as needed, until it becomes a habit.

Lesson Nineteen: You Don't Need To Rush The Big Decisions.

Don't rush the process. Allow yourself to grow at your own pace. Stop comparing your life to what other people are achieving. - Unknown.

As a child, I couldn't wait to become an adult. Now that I am an adult, I don't know why I was in such a rush! I love the freedom and responsibility but there are times when I miss being a carefree kid.

As adults there are so many decisions we need to make each day. Some may seem insignificant (what to wear, what route to drive, what to watch on TV) in comparison to the big decisions you need to make throughout your life such as marriage, children or no children, where you'll live, the job you'll be in, or the business you'll create. These decisions can very well change the trajectory of our lives – for better or worse depending on how you feel about the decision you've made.

Since I started writing this book at twenty-nine, Jesse and I have discussed some of these bigger life decisions and made changes. In the past year we've both changed jobs, purchased a house together, got a second dog, and decided we wanted to start a family. I can tell you with complete certainty that there was no way I was ready to settle down like that during my twenties. I wanted to live life and have some life experiences before I even considered starting a family.

You may look around at others and see how they're living their lives.

Maybe you yearn for what they have. Maybe the thought of having what they have sends you into a panic. When it comes to the big decisions about whether you'll get married, have a child, buy a house, travel, or whatever it might be you're allowed to think it over and do what is right for you. You can do things in your own time. The only timeline to follow is the one you create for yourself. You're allowed to use society's expectations as a guide, but you don't have to follow it to a tee if that isn't what you want. At the end of the day you are living with the choices you make not them.

Making a life changing decision based on what others are doing isn't the best idea. I've been in group conversations which have focused on being a mum and having children. I felt excluded from the discussion because it wasn't something I had gone through or could relate to. That feeling of exclusion was not enough for me to consider starting a family. Basing a big decision on what others are doing, what you think you should be doing, or just to feel like you belong may feel like an easier option but is it the decision you really want to live with? It's okay to take time to figure out what YOU want and while others may not approve, support, or understand your decision... they don't have to! I won't have a child because someone else tells me I should. I would have to live with that choice and that child, not them.

Before you make a big decision, I encourage you to check in with yourself and ask whether your decision is based on how you feel or how others want you to feel about it. If you're basing your decision on what others are doing, ask yourself why do you want it? For instance, if your friends are having kids and you want a kid to fit in, is that the only reason? If so, it might not be the right time for you. It may sound like a cliché but only you know when you're ready. You may never be 100% ready but if you're excited about the thought of the big decision coming to fruition, that's a good indicator.

If you are feeling unsure of what you should do I encourage you to imagine life having made the decision to do it, and then imagine life having made the decision not to do it. Which one do you feel more aligned with? Which one excites you and which one fills you with dread? You could also try to find a middle ground where you can have part of it now and other parts later.

I hope that when you feel pressured to make a big decision that you can take a moment to pause and think about what you want to do. The pressure is either imposed on us or self-imposed and most of the time, we don't need to make a decision as urgently as we might think. Give yourself time to think and make the best decision you can, with the information you have at your disposal.

Affirmations:

1. I am allowed to take my time.
2. I am making the best decisions for myself.
3. I am allowed to consider my thoughts and feelings when making a decision.
4. I trust my decision-making skills.
5. I am good at making decisions.

Journal Prompts:

1. Do I feel like I've rushed any major life decisions? Why or why not?
2. Did I rush a decision because I felt pressure from those around me?
3. When making big decisions, do I give more weight to the opinions of others or my own opinion? Why?
4. Am I able to stand behind a big decision I make even if others may disagree with it?

5. Do I take my own values into account when making major life decisions?

Activities:

1. Reflect on a time where you let others decide for you. How did you feel during that process? Did you try to voice your opinion or were you passive in the decision-making process?
2. Reflect on a time when you made your own decision and stood firmly behind it. Did you consult others during the decision-making process? If so, how did that feel?
3. Reflect on your decision-making process. Do you have someone or a group of people who you consult with when making a major decision? Do you feel pressured to make a decision based on their input or are you able to stand firm on your decision irrespective of their opinions?

Lesson Twenty: When Life Diverges From The Plan, Change It.

You can have a plan, but you have to be flexible. Every day is unpredictable, and you just have to go with the flow. - Jane Krakowski.

Have you ever tried to find something and were adamant that the thing was lost – only to find it was hiding in plain sight the entire time? Whenever this happens to me I often feel baffled. How could I not see what was right in front of me? The short answer is tunnel vision. When we become hyper-fixated on something, our brains drown out anything it deems irrelevant. It's like using a filter to sift through information. You may be looking for one thing when the answer lies elsewhere but because you have the filter on you can't see it.

According to the Oxford Dictionary, a plan is a "detailed proposal for doing or achieving something." Plans are a great starting point to support us in taking action towards achieving our goals. However, they should remain flexible so we can avoid becoming so focused on sticking to the plan that we get tunnel vision and miss seeing the opportunities that could help us along the way.

In my early twenties, I would create plans and want to follow them exactly. I wasn't willing to deviate from the plan, regardless of circumstances. When I travelled by myself, I'd create detailed itineraries. I'd plan out each day and write down a list of activities

I'd want to complete. It didn't matter what the weather was like or whether it was a seasonal activity. I would go. On a visit to Launceston in Tasmania, Australia I wanted to visit a lavender farm. I saw photos of it online and thought it would be incredible to see the colourful purple fields. During my trip a local advised me that the lavender field wouldn't be worth visiting because it wasn't the growing season for lavender. I still made the long drive out to the farm and was disappointed when I saw a brown field instead of the vibrant purple field I was hoping for. Looking out at the field, I could see rows of brown lavender plants that had no flowers on them.

Even with the new information presented to me I still chose to follow the plan and was disappointed by the outcome. I could have listened to the advice of the local and looked up when the lavender field would be in season, making an informed decision instead. I could have filled that time with another activity, perhaps one that was in season. I chose to be stubborn. While I still enjoyed the scenic drive out to the farm, my disappointment was caused by a lack of flexibility and an unwillingness to change my plans. Plans are not permanent yet often they are treated as if they are. As a starting point, plans give us direction and focus. Once a plan is in motion it should be referred to as a guide and changed as needed.

When you make a plan for how you're going to achieve your goal, it's often done before you've started. You forecast the steps you need to take to achieve your goal based on the information you have at that point in time. You may notice that as you move closer to attaining the goal the steps change. This is because we are presented with new information along the way and the original way forward may not be the best option. Variables we hadn't considered or weren't aware of previously, now need to be considered. As we gain experience and insight into what we need to do to achieve our goal, we may find ways to optimise the time and effort spent working on it. If we are closed off to making any changes or deviating from the original plan, we may miss opportunities to streamline our plan. We may get tunnel vision and miss what is right in front of us.

Just as we gain experience as we move through life, we gain experience in pursuit of our goal. A plan allows you to get started and gain momentum, it doesn't mean you need to throw the whole plan out the window. It does mean you should be open to it changing. A change in plan does not represent failure. If anything, it shows your courage to make changes and course correct as necessary. It also highlights that you're making progress and learning.

Flexibility is a skill, not a hindrance. If you look at the stories of people who have reached great levels of success there's a common theme. Their plans changed along the way. They experienced failures yet they didn't allow it to stop them. Instead they adjusted their plan and tried something else, ultimately reaching their goal.

If you are someone who likes to follow plans exactly as they are mapped out, I encourage you to reflect on whether that is working out for you or not. How does it feel when someone wants you to deviate from the plan? Do you tend to feel anxious, stressed, or frustrated at that thought? Would you be willing to be flexible, deviate from the plan, or rewrite the plan entirely if there's a better path you can take?

If you would like to use plans more as a guide my first tip is to remind yourself when you create a plan that it's a guide. Nothing more, nothing less. The purpose of the plan is to help you get started and the steps outlined in the plan are not set in stone. The plan can shrink or expand as needed. It's a supportive tool to help you achieve your goal.

My second tip is to become detached from the plan. The less you have attached yourself to the plan and how seamlessly it works the more comfortable you will be with making edits to it. Remember, you are not a failure if the plan needs to change. It is near impossible to take into consideration every variable which may happen on the path to achieving your goal. The plan cannot take all these variables into account. If you can work with the plan, and go with the flow, and see revisions as an opportunity to learn you will come to realise that you cannot fail by having a plan in place.

When I was twenty-one, my dad and I went to Singapore for a father-daughter trip. My dad had observed my trip itineraries for my solo trips and wanted to show me how he liked to travel. I appreciate that he didn't say that I was overplanning or trying to fill too much into each day, he simply showed me another way. When we were in Singapore, we didn't pre-plan each day. Instead, we woke up and we would find a nearby buffet breakfast to indulge in. Over breakfast, my dad would suggest an area of Singapore to explore, and our day would begin. We began each day with a starting point and where that day would end, we didn't know. I really enjoyed being able to explore without expectations or checking the time. On one of the days, we caught the cable car across to Sentosa Island. We explored the barracks and then we wandered through the shopping complex. We saw a sign promoting Marvel sand sculptures, so we went to check those out. I felt so relaxed during that trip and I was grateful to my dad for showing me that plans are good but when you allow them to be flexible, you can see more of what you want and really enjoy the experience. It's a travel philosophy I use to this day. I've also applied it more broadly in my life because going with the flow was less stressful than trying to stick to an outdated plan.

Having a plan is better than no plan at all. Imagine getting in your car and driving aimlessly, with no destination in mind. While some may see this as being spontaneous, for the purpose of this example it's to highlight that we like to have a sense of direction when we do have a destination in mind. We like to know where we are headed, even if we aren't sure which path we will take to get there. The same applies to having a plan for working towards our goals. It is better to have a plan to guide our action than none at all. Use it as a starting point and from there, be flexible. You cannot account for every variable while planning and if you try to, you'll likely never start implementing the plan. If something isn't working, change it. When you're open to new opportunities rather than being hyper-fixated on trying to execute the plan perfectly, you'll likely find that you reach your goal or outcome faster and in a way you may not have expected.

Affirmations:

1. I am flexible with my plans.
2. I release control and go with the flow once a plan is in motion.
3. I trust that the next best step will be presented to me at the right time.
4. I am not attached to my plans. They are a guide.
5. I am open to new ideas.

Journal Prompts:

1. Do I create plans? If so, how do I use them?
2. Am I willing to use a plan as a guide and be flexible?
3. Am I flexible or do I prefer to follow steps exactly as they are?
4. Have I tried to stick to a plan perfectly? How did the situation turn out?
5. How do I feel when I'm flexible with how a plan is executed?

Activity:

Create a plan for an upcoming weekend or goal. When the time comes and the plan is implemented, observe your behaviour and actions. Do you try to stick to the plan perfectly regardless of what else is happening, or do you go with the flow? Do you find it easier to stick to the plan or to go with the flow?

Lesson Twenty-One: When What If Becomes What Now.

The what-ifs and the should-haves will eat your brain. - John O'Callaghan.

As we go through life we are faced with challenges and opportunities. Both provide us the chance to learn. I feel like I've learned more from my failures and challenges than I have from successes and opportunities. Challenging times ask us to rise to the occasion. We must act, make decisions, and decide whether the thing that is at risk is worth having whether that thing is a goal, a relationship, a business, a career, or something else.

Life isn't linear. There are ups and downs, twists and turns, celebrations and tragedies. While the degree to which each of us experiences the highs and lows may vary, no one is immune. I hope the lessons and experiences I've shared with you throughout this book will bring you some comfort and a fresh or new perspective. Navigating the good times and the hard times isn't straightforward. It can feel lonely, confusing, and overwhelming. There are tools you can use to help you navigate these times and I've shared what has worked for me.

As I was writing this book, Jesse and I went through a challenging time that we had never experienced before. While this event happened after I'd entered my thirties, it taught me a lesson that I knew needed to be included in this book. With respect and consideration for others who have gone through a similar experience, I want to start with a trigger warning. This chapter contains discussion of miscarriage and pregnancy loss. If you or someone close to you has experienced miscarriage or pregnancy loss help is available. Please speak to a healthcare or mental health professional for support. The experience I share is my own and does not constitute professional advice.

At the age of thirty, I found out I was pregnant. I used a few tests to confirm I was pregnant because seeing the two lines for the first time felt surreal. I kept the news to myself for about 20 minutes before sharing it with Jesse. That moment felt surreal, we were both excited, I was crying happy tears and Jesse had the biggest smile. We found out I was pregnant very early when I was around three weeks pregnant. When it was time for our first ultrasound we were both excited because we wanted to see our embryo. At the first ultrasound when I thought I was around eight weeks pregnant, we discovered that the embryo hadn't grown beyond six weeks and there was no detectable heartbeat. My heart sank because I knew that wasn't a good sign. We left that appointment feeling confused and worried. I visited my GP and she recommended I get blood tests done to see if we could find out whether it was a miscarriage or not. Those tests were inconclusive which meant I had to go back for another ultrasound.

I had the next ultrasound roughly two weeks after the first. The ultrasound confirmed what we had feared. I had an incomplete or missed miscarriage. The embryo hadn't grown or developed a heartbeat. Having to sit in uncertainty for those two weeks hoping for the best but anticipating the worst was incredibly hard. I kept jumping between everything will be okay and I know it's over again and again. In a way, I had already begun grieving to help prepare myself for the worst possible outcome.

Now that we had our answer, I returned to my GP the following day to see what my options were for ending the pregnancy. As the miscarriage didn't occur naturally, I needed to help it along. I was given a referral letter to King Edwards Memorial Hospital and told to attend the hospital the following day. A doctor ran through the options, and I had a decision to make. As I had an interstate trip a week later, I opted for the procedure and was booked in the next day. Three weeks after our first ultrasound, it was all over.

I tried to act like I was okay. That I had accepted what had happened. To some degree I had. I also had deeper feelings I tried to conceal. I felt ashamed because I'd had a miscarriage. I wondered what I did to cause it. I felt guilty and upset. Deep down I knew it wasn't my fault. That sometimes these things happen. But I wanted to place the blame on myself. I wanted answers, but none came.

I'm grateful to Jesse, family, and friends who offered compassion and support during that time. I shared my experience on social media. Not to illicit sympathy but to spread awareness of the things we go through behind closed doors. You don't know the silent battles people are facing. During that period of uncertainty, while we waited to find out whether I was having a miscarriage, Jesse and I had weddings to attend. We still went to work and showed up for others as best we could, trying not to let others see what we were going through until we knew for sure what was happening. It wasn't easy but we got through it.

From that experience I learned there are times when you need to sit with uncertainty and how you sit in it is up to you. You can choose to think about the possible outcomes, both positive and negative. Or you can try and focus on each day, trusting that you'll have an answer when the time comes. You can choose to try and control every outcome, or you can surrender and trust. I chose the latter which was not easy but I knew that I had no control over the situation and trying to control the outcome or overthink all the different options was not what I wanted to do. I wanted to focus on my relationship, my mental health (by not overthinking) and work.

And I learned to replace "what if" with "what now".

The what ifs can haunt you if you let them. It's when we look back on the past, hoping for a different outcome. What if that didn't happen, maybe I'd be happier, still in love, in a different place. While hindsight offers us a chance to reflect, you cannot change the past. Dwelling on it only detracts from what you have control over – the present. The longer you reminisce on the what ifs of the past, the longer you're avoiding the present. If you want to change the future, reflect on the past to make changes in the present.

I'm not suggesting anyone boycott the phrase "what if". It can be useful when thinking about your future and possible outcomes. You might want to visualise the positive what ifs. What if I accept this job offer and I thrive in the role? What if I choose to start my business and it is a success? What if I give love another chance and I find my soulmate?

In those examples, the what if question encourages you to change your perspective on the situation. Rather than dwelling on what couldn't work out, you can take a moment to reflect on what could go right instead. This may help you work out whether you're resisting something new out of fear or a genuine concern that it won't work out. Either way, what if allows you to consider alternative outcomes.

There are many variables in life that we simply cannot predict. Using the "what if" question is a quick and powerful tool to use. However, it's important not to get lost in it. If you try to imagine every possible outcome, good and bad, you'd be reflecting for a long time and you still wouldn't be able to capture everything either.

When using "what if" is no longer serves us or simply as an alternative tool for your reflection, try using the "what now" question. The "what now" question is useful for times when you're feeling stuck, stagnant, or have been overthinking a situation. This question can also be used after a situation has happened and you're wanting to work out what the next step is.

Continuing with my miscarriage story, I used the "what now" question to have a conversation with Jesse about what we wanted to do next. I can't recall the exact words from our conversation, but it was along the lines of… "Well, our first try wasn't successful. What now?". The question allowed us to share our thoughts and feelings and to see if or when we might be ready to try again. I used this question as a journal prompt to reflect on how I was feeling after the miscarriage and how I wanted to feel. I reflected on how I wanted to heal, when I might feel ready to try again (if ever), and how I could leave the fears of it happening a second time behind.

Using "what now" allows you to identify the situation, where you are at (emotionally, physically, mentally etc.), where you want to be (the next step), and identify ways to close the gap between where you are now and where you want to be. The "what now" question is a tool. You can use it in a conversation, as a journal prompt, or as an open question to yourself. It allows you to look to the future and decide what you want to do next. It's not intended to suppress your emotions or to help you move forward without processing what has happened.

Affirmations:

1. I look for opportunities in challenges.
2. I am excited about my future.
3. I am grateful for what I have learned.
4. What is meant for me will always find me.
5. I am a solution finder.

Journal Prompts:

1. When you're in a challenging situation, how do you respond? Do you feel stuck where you are? Or do you look for ways to move forward?
2. How much time do you spend reflecting on the "what ifs"?
3. How would you use "what now" in a challenging situation?
4. Reflect on a time when you looked for solutions in a challenging situation. How did you feel?
5. Reflect on a time when you focused primarily on the problems in a challenging situation. How did you feel?

Activities:

1. Reflect on a what if situation. What would have happened if the situation had unfolded differently? What would you not have learned or experienced? Write down things you can be grateful for from that situation.
2. How do you use "what if" most often? Is it looking into the future or is it reflecting on the past? Is it used in a positive or negative way?

Conclusion.

"Don't live the same year 75 times and call it a life." – *Robin Sharma.*

You can choose to live life or you can choose to exist. The choice is yours. Life affords us an opportunity to grow and evolve if we are open to doing so. Each of us grows and evolves in our own way and in our own time so there's no need to rush. There is no age limit on having fun or trying something new. Our only limits are self-imposed.

When I started on my personal development journey it dawned on me that I was in control of my life. I could choose whether I wanted to live the same life on repeat or I could make a conscious decision to grow and evolve. Seven years on and I am glad I choose the latter. My growth and evolution to date hasn't always been pain free. Growth comes with some hard to learn lessons, some hard to accept lessons. It comes with goodbyes, both of others in your life and the person you thought you were. Yet I would rather that than live the same year on repeat. You too have that choice.

Chances are you're not the same person you were five years ago. Growing up and time passing are seemingly obvious reasons why you wouldn't be the same person but that's not all there is to it. Your lived experiences including the highs and the lows have played a big part in creating the version of you that lives and breathes in this present moment.

Whether you're just beginning your personal development journey or you've been on the journey for a while, you may have times when you resist growth. Realising you have control over your life and the decisions you make can be daunting. Doing the inner work can be confronting. Along the way you may discover parts of yourself that you don't want to deal with. Whether it's a deeply rooted subconscious belief, a traumatic experience, or being honest with the kind of life you want to live you may not be ready to process it.

If you are wanting to deal with or process trauma or a massive life event, you may want to speak to a professional who can assist you in working through the experience. Asking for help or seeking out professional guidance is not a sign of weakness. Whilst your personal development journey is yours, you are allowed to ask others for help. It isn't a journey that you need to undertake alone. Personal growth and evolution can be achieved by way of investing time, energy, and money into education, accumulating knowledge, learning a new skill, starting a business, seeking out different relationships, and so forth. An example of your willingness to grow lies in this very book you are choosing to read.

You don't need to be the person you were previously. If someone tells me that I've changed I take it as a compliment. I like to think it means I'm moving forward and evolving rather than standing still.

I've gone from crying on bedroom floor as a newly twenty-year-old to a woman in her early-thirties who is content. When I reflect on how I've changed in the past decade, I am filled with joy and gratitude. At twenty, I was grieving what felt like the loss of my youth. I wasn't sure what my twenties had in store for me and that filled me with excitement and fear.

During my early twenties, I enjoyed staying up late and going out with friends. The mornings were rough but that was what coffee was for, right? I was studying at university and working part time at a supermarket. In my free time, I was going on road trips and interstate trips by myself to explore new parts of Australia. I gave dating a go and discovered that being by myself was better than being in a relationship with someone who I wasn't going to develop deep feelings for.

Friendships were formed and lost, I had my first car accident and purchased a brand-new car. I lived overseas for 6 months and returned home to meet the love of my life shortly after. I discovered the beauty in having a plan and being flexible with how it unfolded. I started to look for opportunities rather than focusing on the obstacles and through mindfulness practices such as yoga, journaling and writing, I learned to be grateful for who I was and what I had in my life.

At twenty-four, I moved out of home and created a home with Jesse in his newly built house. Together, we travelled interstate and overseas. At twenty-five, we got our first dog, a border collie named Lana. I changed jobs a few times and discovered personal development. At twenty-five/twenty-six, I started to work on my mindset, delve into spirituality and discover new hobbies such as reading, writing, yoga and hiking. I started to set goals for myself, one of which was writing a book which I self-published at twenty-eight.

That brings me to The Year I Was a Shadow of Myself. I loved, lost and experienced the depths of grief. It was during this year, I discovered an inner strength I didn't know I had. I was brave enough to sit in my feelings and not suppress them. My core values and beliefs were strengthened during this time as I remembered who I was and what I stood for.

As I entered my thirties, I was able to reflect on how I got to this point in life. The version of me that currently exists is thanks to all my yesterdays and how I navigated the opportunities and challenges presented to me. As much as we all want a good or possibly easy life, I am grateful for the challenges because without them, I wouldn't have grown as a person. I wouldn't have made changes or looked inward to question if I was happy in areas of my life or what I needed to change to be. I am creating a life that I love and am grateful for each day.

I am still learning and growing, even in my thirties. I don't believe the life lessons stop, they simply change as we move through different decades or periods of our lives. As you evolve, so will the lessons you go through.

Entering your twenties is an exciting time in your life. It affords you freedoms you didn't have as a child and you get the opportunity to be who you want to be. You begin to find your own way in the world and become less dependent on others.

During this decade, you'll begin to discover what your core values are which will help you make decisions and know what you stand for. There will be things which are new and unknown, I hope you have the courage to say yes when it feels right. No can be a reflex response and not a true reflection of what you want to do.

You may feel pressure from yourself or others to have it all figured out. Give yourself grace to be a work in progress and figure things out as you go. Try to build and nurture friendships and relationships that bring out the best in you and you, them.

There will be moments when you'll be tempted to act petty or like an asshole. If it goes against who you are as a person, try to catch yourself before you act or say something you may regret. Words and actions cannot be undone and if you can find ways to not respond impulsively, it will work in your favour.

As much as it may hurt to say goodbye or to watch a friendship or relationship end, I hope you are brave enough to know when it's time to let go. When one door closes, another opens. Equally as important, trust your intuition. There will be moments in your life that defy logic. You just know. Go with it, you don't always need to explain it to others.

As you move through your twenties, you'll begin to establish yourself as your own entity. You'll be more certain of who you are and what you want. During this evolution, you'll want to focus on what you can control. There are so many things in life that are beyond our control and trying to control the uncontrollable is near to impossible. Focus your energy on controlling what you can such as your actions, input and behaviour.

It's okay to make mistakes. Adults are not perfect beings. If you are trying something new, you'll likely make mistakes. See it as an opportunity to learn rather than as a reason to give up. Instead of relying on motivation to get things done, become disciplined. Create routines that support your goals and the lifestyle you want to create. This will increase your output and reduce the amount of time you spend trying to convince yourself to take action.

Give yourself permission to create boundaries and set standards for yourself. Boundaries can be temporary or longer lasting. It may feel uncomfortable communicating your needs but people cannot read your mind.

Once you've embarked on your personal development journey, you might wonder, when will it end? Is there are destination to reach? In my opinion, there isn't a destination and the length of your journey is personal to you.

When making decisions, try to think about your own needs first. Others don't care as much as you think they do and if you're making decisions based on what you think someone else may say or respond, you may be missing out on something wonderful. If it feels right to you, take the chance. You can take the opinions of others into consideration when making decisions but it's your life. You get to make final decision and deal with the consequences.

Once you've established yourself as your entity, it's time to grow and evolve. When you take responsibility for your actions, you put yourself back into the driver's seat of your life. From here, you own the choices you make and actions you take.

I want you to remember that your weight does not define your value as a human being. In a world where we're constantly told how we should look, act and dress, find ways to be true to yourself. The aim is to be confident and content in who you are and speaking from experience, reaching a "goal weight" won't give that to you.

If you get the chance, I hope you are bold enough to pack a suitcase and travel. Open your horizons, live on borrowed time and gain a deeper understanding and appreciation of the world around you. Travel may not be the cheapest activity but the memories you'll make and growth you'll experience are more than worth the financial investment.

Our time here is finite and the sooner you start investing time, money and energy into yourself, the better. Whether it's investing in personal development courses, learning a hobby or trying something new, you are worth investing in. You deserve to focus on yourself and be selective on how you spend your time, money and energy.

When it comes to the big life decisions, the only timeline you need to focus on is yours. If you don't feel ready, don't succumb to the opinions of others. You'll need to live with the consequences of your actions, not them. Equally, when a plan goes awry, take it as an opportunity to pivot. Use a plan as your guide and be open to opportunities. You never know what you'll find and what feels like an obstacle could be exactly what you needed at that time.

And lastly, consider replacing "what if" with "what now" when you're in a challenging situation. Rather than focusing your time and energy on thinking of what could have happened instead of what did, shift your attention to what can you do about it now that it's happened. This mindset shift will help you as you move through life.

I am learning to let go of the desire for my life to look a certain way by a certain age. Success is subjective and it doesn't have a used by date. I used to over-commit to events and then cancel last minute. These days, I try to honour my commitments and cancel only when there is an emergency or something unexpected has come up.

Please don't be afraid of evolving and growing as a person. It's healthy and natural. You are allowed to change as you move through different periods in your life. You do not need to fit in a box. You are allowed to be a multi-faceted and ever-changing person, if you so choose. Perhaps you've settled or hidden parts of yourself to fit in. It's easier and sometimes safer to mould into the version of yourself that others expect you to be. What is the cost of hiding parts of yourself? Is it a price you're willing to pay?

You don't need to limit yourself. You can be whoever you want to be. You are allowed to grow, expand, and evolve without having to justify yourself to others. This may be something you've experienced, are currently experiencing, or have yet to go through.

We often look to others for validation. At the end of the day, we know how we feel about a situation. Sometimes, that feeling is intense and other times, it's like a whisper. It's there, you just need to be willing to trust yourself.

I hope you've taken what you've need from the lessons and reflected on your life throughout.

Whether you're about to begin your twenties, you're in the thick of it, are about to enter your thirties or another decade altogether, I hope you found comfort in the words I shared in this book. There may be lessons you've yet to experience and maybe you never will. These lessons are a snapshot of what I've learned in life so far and the ones I thought would be most advantageous to share. They're not intended to be a checklist or a source of comparison. Rather, I intend for this book to be a guide and something for you to turn to if you're in a similar situation and unsure of what to do next.

Your journey, experiences, stories, and memories are unique to you. Your life is your own masterpiece and you can use whatever you like to create it. You can even start again with a new canvas and different equipment. There's no set of rules you need to follow which can feel liberating and terrifying at the same time.

As a work in progress you're able to change, grow, and evolve. If you feel stuck, stagnant, or like you've lost a part of your self-identity, reclaim it. Try new things, explore, experiment, and discover a new version of yourself.

I wish you all the best as you continue to embark on the beautiful journey we call life.

Acknowledgements.

Writing this book has been a labour of love. None of it would have been possible without the love and support from my incredible husband, Jesse. From sounding board to my unofficial editor, his support and trust in me is unwavering. His belief in my words and the stories I've shared is unwavering and for that, I am eternally grateful.

To our baby boy, while he may not be earthside just yet, he's already taught me so much about patience, tuning into my body and slowing down. He inspired me to make finishing and publishing this book a priority.

To my mum and dad who are two of my biggest supporters. Their belief, love and support has helped shape the woman I am today. Wherever I go, I know they're just a phone call away and will always be there to celebrate the highs and lows of life.

To my sister, Em and her husband, Jacob. Your support means so much. It's been incredible to watch your evolutions both as a couple and individuals over the years. You are the definition of soulmates.

To my editor, Kerryn (@kerryn.trisha), thank you. From the moment we started voice-noting, I knew we had to work together on this project. Your skills are magnificent. I appreciate your insight, patience and questions which helped me to make this book the best it could be.

To Danni of @danichecreative, thank you for capturing my author bio photo. Having had the pleasure of work with you, I appreciate your passion for photography and diving beneath the surface during your branding sessions to get to know your client, their story and for capturing it all so beautifully.

To my friends and family, thank you. For those who have supported my growth and been part of my evolution, I appreciate you from the bottom of my heart.

To you, the reader. Thank you for purchasing a copy of this book and for supporting my dream. It's my hope that you will continue to grow and evolve into the best person you can be. While I can share these lessons with you, I hope you're brave enough to grow through what you go through and that this book is only a bookshelf away.

About the Author.

Tash Leam lives in Perth, Western Australia with her husband, Jesse, and two dogs, Lana and Skye. At the time of publication, Tash and Jesse are expecting their first child, a baby boy.

Tash is a personal development enthusiast who enjoys a wide range of hobbies. Her first book *From Human Doing to Human Being* was released in 2021 and is available in paperback and eBook formats. The book is available on Amazon.

You can connect with Tash on Instagram @tash_leam.